The Toddler Years

Also by Paulien Bom and Machteld Huber:

Baby's First Year: Growth and Development from 0 to 12 Months

Paulien Bom and Machteld Huber

The Toddler Years

Growth and Development from 1 to 4 Years

Written in cooperation with Guus van der Bie,
Anneke Maissan-van der Hoeven and Toke Wormer-Bezuijen

Floris Books

Translated by Tony Langham and Plym Peters

Originally published in Dutch under the title
Groeiwijzer van één tot vier jaar by Christofoor in 2006

First published in English by Floris Books in 2009.

© Uitgeverij Christofoor, Zeist 1997
English version © Floris Books, Edinburgh 2009

British Library CIP Data available

ISBN 978-086315-691-5

Printed in Great Britain by
Athenaeum Press, Gateshead

Contents

About the Authors

Guus van der Bie is a family doctor at the Centre for Anthroposophical Health Care in Zeist, Holland, where he runs a clinic for children. He is also active in anthroposophical medical research and training.

Paulien Bom-Bos worked for years as a nurse at an anthroposophical health centre in Amsterdam and at the clinic of the Centre for Anthroposophical Health Care, Zeist. She now works as a publicist.

Machteld Huber trained as a GP and worked at a centre for preventive medicine from an anthroposophical perspective. Together with others, she founded the Dunamis Food Institute, of which she was the director until 2000. She now works at the Louis Bolk Institute in Driebergen, where she researches the health benefits of organic food, and organizes courses and training for medics.

Anneke Maissan-van der Hoeven worked as a nurse for twenty-two years, caring for parents and their children at the Centre for Anthroposophical Health Care, Gouda. Since 1981, she has worked there as psycho-social worker, and is actively involved in biographical counselling, biographical courses and developmental issues.

Toke Wormer-Bezuijen works as a nurse practitioner at the Centre for Anthroposophical Health Care in Zoetermeer. She runs courses on the development of infants and toddlers, as well as antenatal classes. She also works as a therapist, providing physical and palliative treatments in her own practice, as well as at the Centre for Anthroposophical Health Care in Leiden.

Preface

Shortly after the publication of *Baby's First Year: Growth and Development from 0 to 12 Months* we were asked to write a follow-up book about the next stages of a child's life. *Baby's First Year*, which had initially been written for use in anthroposophical health centres, proved to meet a much wider need for guidance on this subject, and so we agreed to produce a second guide. This book covers a much longer period of time — the next three years of a child's life.

From the first to the fourth year of life the child's upbringing requires an increasing amount of attention, as well the day-to-day care of diet and practical care that he receives. As well as discussing the basics of dietary requirement and care, the subject of parenting is also dealt with in detail.

With the birth of a child, you are born as a parent, and the learning process of bringing up your child begins. The practical decisions you make as parents are personal choices, and this applies even more to the ways in which you decide to raise your child. The ideas on parenting that you find in this book may or may not be ways in which you choose to raise your child. The authors have tried to present the information in such a way that the reader feels free to make their own choices, and to develop new opinions. We hope we have covered the fundamental basics parents need to do this.

The Toddler Years is meant as a guide for parents, rather than an all-in-one package of solutions. It certainly does not claim to be comprehensive. We hope to encourage parents to become more aware of what we feel are important considerations when raising a child, and of their own values, in a process of constant growth, and to reflect these values in the way they raise their children. When we refer to 'parents', we are addressing the person who is raising the child.

The Toddler Years starts by discussing general viewpoints on parenting and the various aspects of the development of a child. It then deals with more specific issues of caring for a toddler, and works through these different issues in a practical way, for all four successive stages of development. Finally, there is a chapter about some of the common problems that occur in the life of young child — illnesses and other concerns.

This book was developed jointly by five authors, doctors and nurses. In addition, there is a contribution from dentist Peter Borm. The final editing was done by Paulien Bom and Machteld Huber. Detailed comments on the text were provided throughout the writing process by a group of mothers, nurses, doctors, paediatricians and dieticians. We are extremely grateful to them for their contributions.

In particular, we would like to thank the employees of the Uitgeverij Christofoor once again for their cooperation in writing this book, a joint publication by Christofoor and Dunamis.

On behalf of the authors,
Machteld Huber, M.D.

For the revised fourth edition

When the fourth edition was published we thought it was time to take another critical look at the content, to clarify it where necessary and to update it with any new ideas. This resulted in a number of minor changes, which in our view make it fully up to date. We would like to thank the various experts who provided us with valuable feedback.

On behalf of the authors,
Machteld Huber, M.D.
Driebergen, May 2003

1. Important Points to Consider

A warm nest

A child cannot really flourish without a 'warm nest' in which to grow. Love is the most important ingredient for this. The love and encouragement a child receives will enable him to develop bonds with the people around him, to feel safe and to go out into the world full of confidence.

By a 'warm nest' we mean physical warmth, as well as the loving 'warmth' of the family around him. A small child needs physical warmth to thrive; he should be dressed so that he feels comfortably warm all

over, and therefore feels happy in himself.

Sometimes it can feel as if bringing up a child, and setting rules and boundaries, conflicts with the qualities of love and warmth. When setting boundaries, you have to show strength and decisiveness, while love and warmth are usually associated with softness. However, love for a child also means providing a safe and clear environment by being strong and decisive when necessary, and this is by no means always fun.

Another essential element in providing a 'warm nest' can be expressed very well by an Australian proverb: 'The best things you can give your child are roots and wings.' When both of these aspects are provided for the child from a young age, by giving warmth, clarity and safety on the one hand, and by allowing him space to discover the world on the other hand, you will achieve a good balance.

Everything in its own time

It is vitally important for the toddler's progress that they are given enough time to progress through each stage of development thoroughly. Every stage signifies a breakthrough, and in that sense they can be compared to a birth.

For the birth of a child, we know that pregnancy requires a certain amount of time for a baby to arrive safely and healthily. If the pregnancy lasts much more or less than forty weeks, problems arise, some of which are immediately visible.

In going through the various stages of a toddler's development, the issues of arriving too early or too late are not so clearly visible. A child who cannot yet walk by himself but is placed in a baby-walker will not develop visible defects straightaway, but he may miss out on thoroughly working through each aspect of the crawling stage, which are very important for development.

During the stages of being a toddler, the child gets to know the world

around him through all his senses. The toddler masters the world by feeling, tasting, listening and, above all, by moving. It is important for the toddler to have a broad range of experiences using his whole body. If he moves on to the next stage too quickly — a stage that is more involved with understanding — the time for developing a healthy body can be jeopardized.

The art of raising children is to find the healthy middle ground between providing too much stimulation and too few challenges. These days we are inclined to try to speed up development, particularly intellectual development. This leads to the essential physical stages of infancy being neglected. And, at the end of the day, we need more skills in life than just intellectual skills.

A toddler needs protection

For toddlers, impressions penetrate much deeper than for adults. A toddler is 'open': he has not yet built up the buffer of understanding that an adult uses to make sense of the things he sees and experiences. For a toddler, everything penetrates so deeply that it permeates through to the physical level. It is partly because of this that experts consider the first three years of a child's life to be the most vulnerable and important for the child's development, both for their health in later life and for their psychological well-being. During these years the child is dependent on his parents, who see what he needs and protect him as far as possible from undesirable stimuli and experiences.

'Real' experiences

In order to make healthy progress it is important that the toddler has the opportunity to experience a sufficient number of 'real' experiences. By this we mean experiences in which the child learns something new from direct interaction with the world around him, and which make a positive contribution to his development.

In the first instance, these are all the sensory experiences that the child receives through the eyes, ears, nose, mouth and skin. Real things are the smell of the woods, the feelings of cold sand or rough stones, biting an apple, listening to the wind or a bird, or to someone singing a song. Real experiences include things like falling over and getting up again; climbing and clambering; balancing on a little bicycle and building tall towers out of blocks; sitting down at the table feeling very hungry when you have been for a long walk; feeling wet and cold when it's raining, and then warming up by a fire; or shedding big, fat tears when it's not you but your sister who is allowed to look at the beautiful picture book in the cupboard.

If you concentrate only on providing happy experiences for the child, this will hinder the development of his social skills. In addition, there is a danger that the child will miss out on the intensity and challenges of life, in which good things and not-so-good things alternate; he may unconsciously seek more and more pleasant experiences to compensate for that lack.

Inevitably, in addition to the 'real' experiences that promote health, children will also have a considerable number of unhealthy 'unreal' impressions and experiences. The child will receive many unnatural impressions through the eyes, ears, skin, mouth and nose. Odours are often chemical, sounds mechanical, orally the child will taste synthetic colourants and flavourings; with his eyes the toddler will often see more than he can cope with, while the skin will feel materials that are far from natural. If it is possible for the child to have a sufficient number of 'real' experiences, as well as 'unreal' experiences, this will provide a strong basis for health and further development.

Long live the imagination!

The imagination is a rich source of strength, which can flourish in any child who has the space to play to his heart's content. If you, as an adult, have retained something of this imagination from your own childhood years then you are lucky. Imagination is an invaluable resource throughout life, for example, when bringing up children. It allows you to be creative in difficult situations and to manage during tricky times, perhaps when you're struggling on a tight budget or when work is getting you down. It allows the originality that exists within everyone to come into its own, and to brighten up their life. We believe that there are many factors of contemporary life that can inhibit imagination, particularly during childhood, and that therefore prevent children from developing fully.

Bringing up children in your own way

Every child is different and no two parents are the same. Therefore there is no *one* particular method of raising children that suits everyone, and in difficult situations there is never *one* standard solution.

The danger of relying completely on someone else's method of bringing up children, or on other people's opinions, is that you deny your own feelings and your own ability to make judgments: you short-change both yourself and your child. One fundamental piece of advice that underpins any guidance on parenting is to observe things closely: see how your child reacts to what you do as a parent; look at yourself and listen to your own personal needs. Bringing up children involves a natural progression and every parent will make mistakes. For most parents, having a child is a leap into the unknown, and at times you will feel that you don't know what you're supposed to be doing.

Bringing up children is not a matter of avoiding what is wrong, but of doing what you think is right, even if you may be unsure about it. When raising children, there's a constant tension between trying to get it right and knowing that you will inevitably make mistakes. There is an art to not making unachievable demands on yourself and learning from your mistakes, while at the same time knowing that you will probably make them again. Ultimately, everyone has to learn how to be a parent.

Doing and imitating

In order to learn human skills, a child needs a human example. Infants and toddlers are open to everything that is happening around them, and they often imitate these things as they are playing, quite unnoticed. Therefore the example you give as a parent is the most basic aspect of bringing up children. They not only imitate *what* you do but also see *how* you do things, and the more you are able to carry out tasks with care, love and enjoyment, the more positively this influence works. This involves a lot of thought and practice, because no parent has the natural capacity to behave in this way all the time.

Every child has his own destiny

Children from the same family are often very different. Upbringing and heredity are not wholly decisive: the child also has his own individual 'spark' that becomes increasingly visible during the course of childhood. Every person has his own destiny, in which predispositions, abilities or inabilities and illnesses play a role. A happy, sunny, easygoing disposition can predominate in one child, while another child may be prone to illness, not feeling comfortable in himself and being difficult. One child can be easy to relate to because of his very nature, while with another you will constantly come up against a brick wall; and again and again you will feel that you are not responding correctly. Knowing that this is partly the child's destiny can give you a sense of calm and acceptance, particularly during difficult times. You cannot prevent all the problems that a child will encounter with loving care and a good upbringing; the child's upbringing is not necessarily to blame when a child has problems.

2. The Toddler's Development

The development of a small child takes place in accordance with certain natural laws. Because every child is different, the times and the order in which these stages of development take place may differ enormously.

The key word in the toddler's development is 'movement.' A child gets to know herself and the world through movement. She learns what is here and there, in front and behind, above and below, and gets to know her own place in space. She learns to understand concepts such as heavy and light, soft and hard. The child learns that her actions have consequences by doing things, and she acquires a sense of cause and effect.

All these experiences will help the child to develop three important human skills: walking, talking and thinking. She masters these skills in infancy and during the toddler years. To some extent, they are learnt at the same time, and to some extent, one after the other in the order indicated above.

The people in the small child's environment play an important role, first of all because of the example they give, or rather the example they are for the child. It is partly from following this example that a child learns to roll over, pick up objects, crawl, sit and stand during the first year of life. In addition to having an example to follow, the child needs opportunities and challenges so that she can become more and more skilled in her movements: running, climbing, cycling, throwing and catching. If the challenges are varied and appeal to every aspect of the child, she will be able to thoroughly master the skills that she needs to acquire in the first years of her life.

For the sake of clarity, we discuss the toddler's development in a number of separate chapters, although everything is interrelated during the first years of life and you cannot really distinguish between what is psychological and what is physical. In addition to motor development and speech and cognitive development, we will discuss social and emotional development and the development of the will. For most skills, general ages are indicated. If a child does not comply with the average and, for example, learns to walk very late, it may be that she is simply in no hurry to do this and you have to give her all the time she needs; she will learn to when she's ready. However, it can also be a sign that she isn't progressing healthily, and in that case, intervening in good time can be vitally important. That is why it's essential for children to be seen regularly at a child health clinic.

Apart from the fact that it's important to closely observe how a child is progressing and whether she complies with the statistical norms, it's just as fascinating to see *how* the child is doing these things, as this reveals her own individuality. One child may learn to walk suddenly at a later age, while another child may want to start walking very early and only learn to after falling down and getting up again endlessly.

Physical development

It is easy to read the physical development of the child from the changes in her figure. A one-year-old still has a babyish figure, even though the child may already be able to stand and walk. In comparison with the rest of her body her head is still very large, a quarter of the entire body length; the child is 'top heavy.' At this age she does not yet have an obvious neck. The large head is placed more or less directly on top of the torso. The whole body is round and soft with little cushions on the hands and folds at the wrists. This starts to change at eighteen months; the ratios slowly change as the head grows less in relation to the rest of the body.

The figure of the toddler starts to emerge at about two and a half years and this lasts until approximately the age of five. The head now accounts for one fifth of the body length and some of the neck becomes visible so that the head is separated from the rest of the body. The torso has grown significantly, although the legs usually haven't grown much. At this stage, the large, round, soft chest and tummy area is striking and there is not yet a waist.

After the child's fifth year, the emphasis is on the growth of the legs and feet. The child's foot is naturally flat and unformed until about the fifth year. The legs are not straight, as they will become at the end of the toddler years, and slight deviations in shape are normal. At eighteen months many children become bow-legged, and then at the age of three they can look more pigeon-toed.

Children have a very physical focus. They need a lot of physical contact and really want to get to know their own bodies. You can fulfil this need by giving your child lots of cuddles, and by giving her the opportunity to discover herself from top to toe, for example, in the bath. This is discussed in detail in the chapter on ensuring a healthy sexual development (p. 63). Above all, the child will get to know her body by using it.

Motor development

When she reaches the age of one, the small child has usually reached the first milestone in motor development: she can stand and walk along the edge of a playpen or furniture. Some children will even be able to walk on their own. After this, the child learns to move more and more proficiently. Initially she will move only forwards, but gradually the child will develop a sense of what is happening to the side of her, and eventually of the space behind her. During this period, she will tend to carry out movements symmetrically and use the right and left hands alternately, often to pick things up.

From the age of three the child will start to develop a preference for right or left, a process known as 'lateralization.' The pattern of movement then becomes asymmetrical and the child learns, for example, to stand on one leg. This preference for the use of right or left is not only restricted to the hands and legs, but will also affect the ears and eyes. In most cases this means that from the age of three a child is either right-handed and uses the right leg, or left-handed and uses the left leg, but these can also be combined, for example, a child may be right-handed and left-footed. The right or left eye and the right or left ear also become dominant. For example, this is expressed in the phenomenon that a child will always hold the telephone receiver against the right (or left) ear.

The fine motor skills also gradually develop. This involves exploring and feeling everything and picking up small objects with the thumb and index finger. The child slowly learns to play with building blocks,

eat with a knife and fork, drink from a beaker by herself, and undo laces and buttons. By the age of four these motor skills have developed to such an extent that the child is able to dress herself or put together a train track.

You can see the motor development of the child as learning to deal with gravity. The child stands up against the force of gravity. In order to be able to carry out all the movements properly, the senses must work together well and in a coordinated way. In adults this coordination is developed to such an extent that you no longer think about all the senses that play a part in every movement: seeing a step from the corner of your eye and raising a foot automatically so as not to stumble over it; walking while you're hold-

ing on to something; walking and looking round at the same time; kicking a ball without falling over … These are all skills which have become automatic in adults but which a child has to learn by doing them. Therefore it's essential that the child has ample opportunity to move around. The greater the possibilities, the more skilfully and dexterously the child will be able to deal with her body.

Speech development

Speech usually starts to develop between the first and second years of childhood. The groundwork has already been done in the first year of life through the adult talking to the child and singing songs to her.

The first year is sometimes described as the musical-rhythmic period because the child has a particular affinity with the melodious, rhythmic elements of language at this stage rather than for the meaning of words. This affinity continues after the first year, but in addition, more 'verbal' interest develops, and the child learns to understand and use many words.

In the early stages of infancy, all children all over the world use the same general burbling language. Afterwards, a predisposition for the mother tongue develops and this burbling becomes more specialized. Only those sounds that form the basis of the mother tongue are retained. The individual words the child learns relate to the people, things and activities in her immediate environment, such as Dad, Mum, cat, boom, ball, etc. At first they are pronounced in a very distorted way, and are often only understood by insiders. Gradually the child acquires a larger vocabulary and can indicate what she means with words.

Before the breakthrough when the child can clearly express what she wants to say, there may be a period where she wants to but cannot yet manage to express herself. This can make her impatient and difficult until the breakthrough when what she *wants* to do and what she *can* do equate.

After mastering the use of separate words, the child starts to talk in short sentences at about the age of two, and this takes her into a completely different area of language. In creating sentences you must involve language structures, which are formed from a huge range of grammatical rules. Obviously the child will not be aware of these rules immediately, but with a good example and by experimenting herself, she will acquire a feeling for them. Mastering the mother tongue and having a varied vocabulary at her disposal are the most important factors in understanding and in learning to think in a balanced way.

By listening carefully to the words your child uses, you can gain an insight into her understanding of the world. This will enable you to assess what you can expect of her and therefore she will respond better to what you ask her to do. During the early stages, a child discovers that everything has a name and only uses nouns; in doing this she is showing that she lives with things that are visible, or in other words, things which 'are.' With the use of verbs, the child shows that she is also learning to understand the concept of action or 'becoming.' This brings with it the first notions of time. With the next stage, when she starts to use adjectives, such as 'beautiful,' 'big' and 'heavy', the child shows that she is working with the shades or qualities of those things. When the child starts to use the word 'I' at the age of about three and gradually learns to distinguish between I and you and mine and yours, she is showing an understanding that other people are independent and separate from herself. Finally, the child starts to use more abstract concepts, such as 'yesterday' and 'tomorrow,' first 'this' and then 'that,' showing that she is starting to develop an understanding of cause and effect.

The most important thing when raising young children is to give a good example when talking. The child will pick things up most easily if you talk out loud (to describe what you're doing) when you are doing things, and in this way explain what he's seeing and experiencing. For example, 'First we will put on your socks and now your trousers.' By

explaining this clearly and enthusiastically, you will help the child to
correctly pronounce the words she
wants to learn. Talking to a child in
babyish, distorted sentences has a
counter-productive effect.

If the child does not pronounce
words properly or form sentences
correctly, you can help her by pro-
nouncing them correctly yourself
without too much emphasis. A child
starts to talk more easily in an environment in which she feels safe and
in which adults react sensitively to
her attempts at speech.

As we discussed earlier, a toddler has a strong sense of the musical aspect of language and responds
in particular to the intonation with
which words are said. When recit-
ing poems and nursery rhymes, most
people automatically use stronger
intonation than in ordinary speech,
and that's why they're so popular.

A child will be able to express
herself and talk to others more effectively if she has been really listened
to — even when she's tripping over
her own words and doesn't get them
completely right. Often you will
know what a child is going to say
because of the gestures she makes,
and it's important to wait patiently
until she's finished with the words.
In addition, listening quietly to what
someone else has to say is a skill
that must be learnt in childhood.
This process can be disturbed by
constant background noise from the
radio, music or TV: the child learns
not to ignore these sounds from an
early age and to simply talk over
them. Constant background music
also means that a child is likely to
talk too loudly.

Cognitive development

The first steps a child takes on the
path to thinking are those of perception and recognition. When
a child reaches the age of one, a
great deal has already happened in
this respect.

You could say that as a result
of perception, a piece of the outside world gains a place in the inner world of the child. In this way,
from a very young age, a child gath-
ers many perceptions of the outside
world through her senses, which
are then assimilated and turned into
inner images.

A small child would experience
all perceptions as being new and
unknown if the memory did not develop. The rattle, the plate of food,
the dog that is seen for the third,
fourth and fifth time gradually become recognized, which is the first
form of memory. Initially these
perceptions are still separate from
each other, but the more a child recognizes, the more events in life fit
together to create a bigger picture.
In this way she gradually starts to
understand the interrelationship
between things. The bedroom door
opens, Mum or Dad comes in, and
the baby's happy laughter shows
that she understands what's going
to happen next. The child then puts

out her arms, clearly showing what she thinks will happen next, and this signifies the beginnings of thought.

In toddlers you can already see signs of higher stages of cognitive development. A toddler goes out to examine the world and make discoveries. She sees through the interrelationships increasingly quickly and her capacity for recognition improves. Up to the age of four or five the child's way of thinking remains linked to her visible reality and the world around her. After this, the ability to create thoughts independently, without having to see anything concrete at that very moment, starts to develop.

In addition to the perceptions through the senses, language is an important foundation for the development of thought. It is also by naming the things around her that the child is able to start thinking.

You could say that thinking involves concepts moving in relation to each other. First the child learns who 'Dad' is and then she learns what the 'bath' is. Then she learns to interrelate 'Dad' and 'bath.' The child can then make the sentence 'Dad bath.' The phrase 'thought process' expresses exactly what is meant here. By thinking, you move around in the world of ideas, and as you think you move along a path. In small children, this path can be followed step-by-step when they are thinking out loud.

In addition to the practical reality that has become an inner experience through their senses, the inner world of a toddler is also coloured by a magical awareness, which characterises this age. This awareness comes from seeing images where reality and the imagination go hand in hand: Father Christmas is on the roof and presents are coming down through the chimney. Witches, giants, gnomes and angels populate the magical world of the child and are realities for her. It's a world that adults sometimes only get a glimpse of, and it's difficult to form a real picture of it. This magical world ceases to exist at some point during childhood. For some children this is a very gradual process and you will hardly notice the change, but for other children it can end very abruptly.

In recognizing and learning to see interrelationships, rhythms and predictability in daily life can be a great help for the child. The more care and attention that can be devoted to this, the more inner security the child develops.

In addition, respect for the magical awareness of the child will help to provide the support and security she needs. By allowing a place for giants, angels, Father Christmas, gnomes and fairies, you share in the toddler's reality, and she will feel understood and recognized.

Social and emotional development

Feelings form the basis for social and emotional development. The most important characteristic of our emotions is that they fluctuate between extremes: pleasant–unpleasant, happy–sad, beautiful–ugly. All our feelings are somewhere on the scale between these extremes and are linked to the basic experiences of pleasure and displeasure. Small children's feelings are focused in particular on the sense of comfort–discomfort, depending on whether the child feels comfortable in her skin. During the course of the toddler's development, these feelings become slightly less dependent on her own body and interact more with the environment around her. Feelings related to sympathy and antipathy start to develop.

In looking at social and emotional development between the ages of one to four, a turning point is reached between the ages of two and a half and three, when the child starts to say 'I.'

During the period before this, the toddler feels at one with the world, and on the basis of that feeling she says 'yes' to everything she encounters. She goes out into the world to explore with enthusiasm. However, this 'yes' feeling and this enthusiasm can change very easily into a 'no' feeling or into sadness: and this is how feelings work in small children. This is the stage when a child can be smiling one minute and crying the next, and a small distraction can be enough to make them smile again.

Another aspect of this period is that the child focuses on herself and is not yet very sociable. She cannot empathise with others because she doesn't yet know that other people also have feelings. Furthermore, she is still completely concerned with experiencing things for herself, and the development of social skills has not yet emerged.

As mentioned above, one important step on the road to self-knowledge is the moment when the child starts to use the word 'I.' At that point she shows that she has developed a very different relationship to the world and to the people around her. The child no longer feels merged with her environment; she now understands that she is a self, separate from the world and other people. This is a completely new feeling. The child learns to evoke this feeling by repeatedly saying 'no,' until the feeling itself exists beyond saying the word 'no.' This progression signals the end of the 'obstinate stage.'

From the age of three onwards, more of a balance between 'yes' and 'no' is achieved. Children become more cooperative, they acquire a feeling for rules and often do their best for others. By the time they go to nursery school you could say that the child has started to experience herself as an individual among other people. She can behave in a social situation; she starts to feel the need to play with other children and is able to do so.

One of the things for which all children have a strong (often social) desire is that they want the world around them to be complete. When something is broken it has to be repaired, and when someone in the family is missing from the table, that person has to be there. If there's an argument or someone is obviously unhappy, the child wants this to be resolved. During the 'no' stage in particular, this desire can seem to be crushed by the opposing force that also exists in all toddlers: the tendency to examine and break things, to experiment and test boundaries. And for this reason, during this stage, it's important to recognize and nurture the opposing desire of 'wholeness.'

If you are able to build up a family culture in which listening to each other, and respect and appreciation for other people, have an important place, and in which all the things in and around the house are treated with care, this above-mentioned social skill is nourished.

In addition, it's important that the child learns to deal with the problems, objections and frustrations that occur in everyday life — both to build up a healthy emotional life and to develop social skills. To name but a few, these include learning to wait and share, learning to deal with jealousy and when things

don't work. These issues are dealt with in more detail later in the book (see p. 37).

Fear

One of the feelings all children are confronted with is fear. This occurs for the first time at about the age of one when the child becomes attached to one person and is afraid to be separated. The extent to which these fears occur differs for every child. It is a sign of a change of awareness. The person who is not bringing up the child is identified as a stranger and is rejected. The need for security, and to be surrounded by familiar objects proves to be very important at this time. The strong bond that develops between the child and the person raising her becomes visible. As the child becomes better able to bond with others she will feel more secure.

The development of fear is also influenced by the development of the imagination. The first expressions of the imagination occur at about the age of three: a newspaper can suddenly become a tent if you crawl underneath it. In addition to imagination, memory also starts to develop. This combination can mean that incidents in the daytime assume all sorts of grotesque forms at night, which can be frightening. We will explore this further later in the book.

Finally, a child can become frightened if insufficient boundaries are set, and she is able to more or less take control in the home. These are often children who do not appear to accept boundaries, who do not listen attentively and who may act tough, but, as their parents say, they are really very vulnerable and frightened inside.

How can you make a positive contribution to the social and emotional development of the child you are raising?

The most important basis is in providing a 'warm nest.' This means that the child will feel safe, brave enough to go out and explore things, and will build up self-confidence through dealing with resistance.

The example you set is also very important. The child responds strongly to the general mood around her. If you are able to say 'yes' to the things you do yourself, enjoy them and behave positively, this will strengthen the 'yes' feeling of the child. One thing that can help with this is to furnish the toddler's environment in such a way that she can do what she likes and is not constantly confronted with 'no.'

A child also needs to follow the good example of his parents when learning to deal with resistance and frustrations. If you are able to deal with a difficult situation calmly, this gives a much better example to follow than losing your composure at the slightest thing, or waving problems aside because you don't feel like dealing with them.

By being honest with yourself and about the situation, you find the best course to follow. If you are able to transform problems and frustrations into something meaningful, this will help to develop balance in your child's emotional life. It will help them to be able to process the experiences they encounter through life, in which feelings always play a crucial role.

In addition to providing a warm nest and setting a good example, listening and observing carefully are essential, so that you know what is happening in your child's world and, for example, the things he's scared of. You will be able to explain to her what's going on, and this is often the first step to finding the solution to her problems or fears.

Finally, providing a clear lead for the child will help her to develop social skills. By being too strict in approach, the child will adapt too much and become too obedient, because she does not want to jeopardixe your love; and there's a chance that the child's sense of self-worth and respect will be lost.

By not providing a strong enough lead, the child becomes used to doing exactly what she wants, and this can make her fearful and consequently unable to learn to accept rules.

If you can find a middle ground between these two extremes, the child will be able to follow social rules, while her conscience develops on the basis of her own sense of responsibility.

Just as it's important to have a close bond with your child during the toddler years to provide a healthy lead, this bond is extremely important during the later years of childhood. In order to develop strong social skills the child must learn to do what he's asked to, and must learn to control herself if something doesn't go her way. If parents have a close bond with their child, the child will be more likely to obey and to control herself than if this bond has been broken. If there's a close bond, the child will also have the courage to push away, allowing her the chance to get to know herself better.

The development of will

You will constantly come up against the child's will, which is always focused outwards, on doing something. This contrasts with the way of thinking described earlier that focused on the child's inner life.

Up to the age of four, the will is determined mainly by impulse; the child is not yet in control of her own will. It's predominantly the example the child sees in her environment that provides order for her activities.

One stage during which you can clearly see the child's will being driven by impulse is during the obstinate phase, when the child asserts her 'own little will' all the time. On closer inspection, it's clear that she is actually the victim of her 'own

will.' The obstinacy is expressed above all in opposing things for the sake of it, and the child can become completely locked into this pattern. There is actually absolutely no sense of a free human will.

As a toddler does not yet have her own free will, if an adult makes demands of her — especially if she does so forcefully — problems will arise, because the child doesn't yet know how to respond, and so shuts herself off. At this point it will look as if he's quite unwilling to respond or simply not listening, but this response, above all, shows an inability to deal with the demands being made of her. These tricky situations will occur less if the toddler's environment is organised in such a way that she can cope with it enjoyably, and if the emphasis is on things that she *is* allowed to do. The key elements to take from this are good habits and clear boundaries. During the obstinate stage there is quite an art to handling this well, and we will explore this more fully later on (see p. 36).

In relation to the above, problems also arise when you ask a toddler what she wants and, for example, allow her to make a choice from different sandwich fillings. She is unable to make this decision and therefore wants everything, and the situation can lead to a tug-of-war. You cannot ask a toddler to make decisions, because you are asking her to do something she is not yet capable of. It will also use up valuable strength and vitality, which at this stage is needed for healthy physical growth.

You will therefore have to make decisions on the basis of what *you* think is best for the child. This is not easy and for many parents it's certainly not obvious, because discussing things with your child and giving her a choice feels better than limiting him and taking control. You have to be able to see what is best for your child, and you may often not feel sure of this. You must learn to understand that the control you provide gives your child a sense of safety and security.

3. Bringing up Toddlers

Imitation plays an important role in bringing up a toddler. Because a toddler is so open and has such a strong impulse to imitate things, the good example you set should in principle be sufficient for good parenting.

Nevertheless, there are many situations in which the child doesn't copy you and where this openness is not present. A toddler who has to learn to brush his teeth and doesn't want to, will still not want to, even with the example of an adult brushing his teeth. And if you try to achieve your goal by intervening forcefully and becoming angry, it won't work at all. You can feel quite impotent when a toddler doesn't want to eat, sleep, be potty-trained, and so on.

So how do you teach a child something when setting a good example doesn't work and when being strict doesn't either? We would like to answer this question by discussing a number of key points that are particularly important when dealing with toddlers.

Attention

Children need a great deal of attention in all sorts of ways. Firstly, because you can barely leave a toddler alone for a moment for safety reasons. The immediate presence of parents may be slightly less important for a three-year-old toddler, who has developed a slight sense of danger, than for a one-year-old, but with all toddlers you have to grow a pair of very sensitive 'antennae.' It's this sensitive awareness of your child that will tell you, 'Now I have to go and check on him.' In many cases this instinct proves to be justified. It could be precisely at that moment that a biscuit tin is being quietly emptied or the bathroom is being painted with toothpaste, imitating Dad who was painting the shed the day before. The more sensitive the parents' antennae, the more space a child can have to discover the world and play to his heart's content.

In addition to attention to safety, the child also really wants to be noticed. He needs the sincere interest and attention of his parents without having to ask for it. The child will flourish if this attention has a place in the everyday activities of the parents. It's important that he feels this attention physically in the way in which, for example, his nappy is changed or he is cuddled or stroked on the head.

It becomes difficult for parents when many things require their attention. There's an art to multitasking, and it's a learning process. When you are struggling it's often the toddler who decides where your attention must be directed — on him.

Being in a hurry and paying close attention do not go hand in hand. The world of adults is usually organised in such a way that we consciously or unconsciously have all sorts of goals, and the paths to those goal are less important and are often followed in haste.

A toddler works completely differently. Here's one example: I want to go shopping with my child and we first have to put on our coats. For adults, putting on our coats is of secondary importance and we hardly think about it, but for a toddler it's the most important thing there is at that moment. For him it doesn't matter whether it takes one minute or five minutes. The reality for him is that he wants to put his coat on himself and all his attention is focused on that.

Paying attention to your child while doing household chores can go together well. Many parents are inclined to carry out household tasks quickly, while they have a moment, because otherwise there won't be enough time to pay full attention to their child. But for a toddler there are all sorts of things to be discovered and copied in doing housework, and it's wonderful to be able to join in. But as it's simply impossible to do everything together with a toddler, we advise that you alternate doing things together with moments when you each do your own thing.

For a toddler who is used to asking for a lot of attention and receiving it, the moments of time spent apart will at first only be brief, because longer will not yet work. Mark the transitions from doing something together to playing alone, for example by saying, 'First I have to mop the floor, then we'll go and feed the ducks together. Go and play by yourself until I'm ready.'

A child who is not used to playing alone will keep coming back to see if the floor has been mopped or will stand by the front door impatiently. The better you're able to calmly manage the arrangement, the sooner the child will learn to play by himself. However, the promise to go and feed the ducks is part of that deal, even if the telephone suddenly starts ringing.

Hardly any toddler will tolerate a father or mother who is constantly reading, studying, watching TV or on the phone, because the attention is focused on things beyond the child. However, this does not apply, for example, to knitting, ironing, DIY activities or gardening, because these are activities in which you can involve the child. If you don't enjoy these sorts of things, but you do enjoy reading or studying, this can be very frustrating. In that case, arranging for your child to play with another family or a babysitter may give you the room to meet your own needs.

If you are not able to devote enough time to your toddler, this can lead to a negative spiral. Your child will keep pulling on your coat tails until you pay him sufficient attention. If the child has had no reaction or only negative reactions to his request to come and admire his latest building-block structure, he will make himself heard in other ways, for example, by starting to scream or by breaking something. Most toddlers have a whole range of this sort of negative behaviour at hand. When you're tired or overwhelmed, you may only respond when the toddler reaches this last resort, because it's the only way to attract your attention. This in turn elicits more negative behaviour from the child, which takes even more energy, and the circle is complete. This happens to parents again and again, on a small or large scale, because you will always have your hands full looking after toddlers.

This cycle of negativity can become entrenched, because you can't think of a solution other than punishing the child. We will discuss this further in the section on punishments and rewards.

There are a few methods that can help break this type of negative spiral:

• Look back over your day
in the evening. Often it's the
negative things that you notice
first. Try to remember just as
many of the positive moments.

• Praise your child more often than you normally would when you see that he's done something good.

• Make sure you include a few moments of doing something together every day. Look at a book together, sing a song, feed the birds outside with breakfast breadcrumbs, or anything else that the child enjoys. If these moments are repeated every day, the child starts to feel confident that they will occur, without making a fuss.

Rhythm, routine and rituals

There are a number of fixed points throughout the day for every family, such as getting up, getting dressed and eating. The more predictable the course of the day is for a toddler, the more support and security he feels. From recurring activities, such as eating, sleeping and habitual tasks, the toddler gradually starts to understand time and the way in which things are connected. In other words, the child starts to know and understand how life works. The

more inviting and comfortable the environment, the more easily the toddler will take on and become involved in daily family routines.

For a child, it's better if the course of the day is not restrictive like a corset, but has room to breathe. Movement and rest, being alone and together, inside and outside, eating and not eating should alternate in a rhythm, as should (being allowed to) make a mess and tidying it up again (together), (being allowed to) get dirty and then enjoying washing it all off.

The daily routine needs to be regularly revised as the child develops. Here are a few examples.

It's obvious that you dress and undress a one-year-old, but you can certainly encourage a three-year-old to try it himself. A one-year-old will often need a big plate full of food, while a two-year-old can do with much less, so you don't have to give him as much. Looking after small children will take up a large part of the day, but slightly older and more independent toddlers will take up less of your time.

You will need other skills on top of caring physically for the child. Being able to let go becomes important, so that the child can go out exploring by himself and make discoveries. Observing him closely is the best way of getting to know what he needs and what habits need changing.

Habits and rules can become flexible during illnesses and other difficult times. For example, a sick child often needs someone at night. He might want to crawl into bed with his parents or have a drink if he's thirsty because of a fever, and so on. While the child is sick it's perfectly justified to meet these demands. The child may be scared, and the parents too, if the child has a bad cough or fever. And it's difficult to determine when the child is better again and old habits should be restored. Usually there's an undefined period between being ill and being healthy, and this can sometimes lead to stubborn bad habits, such as the child continuing to ask for drinks at night or wanting to sleep with his parents (see p. 137).

Rituals can assume a special place in the family, like well-worn habits. There are few rituals in our contemporary society, particularly as the church no longer plays a central role. Rituals play an important part in the church; they serve to confirm people's religious belief. In the family, rituals can have a similar effect. They can establish a mood of calm and create focus, for example, at the start of a meal or at bedtime. Ordinary life stops for a moment so that your mind can focus on the meal, or so that you can peacefully let go of the day and go to sleep. Children like rituals, they are fond of the repetition and particularly anything visual.

Rituals can differ enormously: one parent may choose to say a prayer at the start of a meal, while another chooses to light a candle or have a moment of silence. To some extent, it depends less on what you do than on how you do it, how faithfully you observe the ritual and how much attention you devote to it. This is all the easier when the family rituals are kept simple and short.

Both habits and rituals are dependent on the family. They often come from your own childhood experiences, from the way other families behave, from views on parenting, and from what suits the family. Your may form new habits after reading a book or talking to fellow parents. In the end, new habits only really become ingrained when they are no longer just ideas, but when they actually start to form part of your daily routine.

Rules and boundaries

Habit and routine mainly affect the realms of the unconscious. Rules and boundaries are used more consciously and can also lead to greater awareness in the child. Rules and boundaries exist first and foremost for the sake of safety and also to ensure that parents and children can live together without friction. When they are clear to everyone and are followed consistently, they provide support and create a sense of order. This also gives the child a sense of safety and security. Rules must always be there for a reason, never as an end in themselves.

When setting rules and boundaries, it's important to bear in mind:

• If you set a rule to forbid something, it's good to show what *is* allowed. Of course, this does not always need to be explained in words. 'That's for you' is clear enough. For example, if a child is not allowed to pull out all the books from the bookcase, organise a shelf for him to stack his own books. Or if a child wants to help clear away, ask him to carry something unbreakable. Try to furnish the house in such a way that many things are possible and allowed.

• What you do, the words you use, and your tone of voice must correspond when you set boundaries. It's confusing for a child if you tell him off, but laugh at the same time because the naughty little thing was really rather sweet.

• You can't expect a toddler to remember rules that were set today, tomorrow and still follow them. Even after removing them ten or twenty times, the books on the bookcase will continue to be tempting, because it's all so exciting. After intervening many times, the child will start to feel that something is not allowed, but that does not mean that the forbidden is no longer attractive; it means that you have to be endlessly patient.

• The more calmly you can lay down rules, the faster they will be accepted. They must first be imposed, before you get really angry.

• It's better to consistently impose a limited number of rules than to occasionally impose all sorts of unclear rules. Parents should decide together which rules they consider important or which rules they would like to teach the child and should then be consistent with enforcing them. You can also tell any older children in the family or a babysitter about any rules and ask them to keep to them too.

If you are struggling to impose rules and boundaries consistently, it may be helpful to take inspiration from the times you are successful in doing so. Usually these will be the rules that relate to immediate safety, for example, the rule that your child may not touch the cooker. Try to adopt the conviction that you are able to express during that moment at other times as well.

Boundaries vary as the child develops. For one-year-olds, they are still very tangible and spatial, such as the crib that the baby cannot climb out of, the playpen, the stair-gate or the harness in the high chair. These sorts of clear boundaries suit a small child because they can be felt and do not require the child to engage their consciousness or memory. The attractive aspect of tangible boundaries is that they are accepted as a given fact, because they are more or less separate from the person who imposes them. Therefore any opposition to this boundary tends to be against the boundary itself rather than against the adult.

As the toddler grows older, these clear physical boundaries increasingly fade. The world becomes larger, the playpen disappears and the child can climb out of his cot. Other boundaries have to be provided now, though they still need to be tangible. For example, if the child is constantly playing with the CD player and is not supposed to, the child will experience being physically picked up and placed somewhere else, where he can do what he likes. At this stage and in this context, parenting is still based on action. It's fine to accompany the physical intervention with words because, over the course of childhood, these words will start to take the place of physical intervention. But during this stage words play a supporting role and should not take the place of action. It's the message conveyed by your actions that will be recognized and experienced as a clear boundary by the toddler. If you become angry or irritated, the child will soon become obstructive and will not be open to what you want.

At about the age of three, a child should start to assimilate some of the rules and boundaries at home,

and it should be possible for the child to obey simply by telling him the rule.

If you become too strict about providing routine and rules, there's a danger it will lead to a punishment regime. Try to stay light-hearted and to look at yourself and at the situations you're in with humour.

Saying no

As soon as a child reaches the so-called obstinate stage, which is usually between the ages of two and three, saying 'no' becomes very common, both for the child and for the parents. The child starts to use the word 'I,' revealing an emerging sense of self. This self-awareness grows by opposing the parents. The child will say 'no' to everything, in extreme cases, even to the things he would like to do.

Although this stage can be complicated and draining, it should be greeted with enthusiasm by every parent. It's a milestone in development, and a stage that no child should miss out on. The ways in which different children experience it and how long it lasts can vary enormously. The extreme 'no' stage starts to fade when the child's sense of identity is strong enough for him to feel less of a need to confront the world around him.

One 'no' often leads to another, and this exchange can pass between parents and children over and over again. Nevertheless, the child will still be most stimulated by confirmation, encouragement and being praised. It's precisely at this age that the child needs this support. For example, if the child resists having his hands washed before dinner and makes a mess with the water but then hangs up the towel properly, it's better to praise him for what he's done well than to grumble about the mess he's made.

In general it's a good thing to distract the child when he's saying 'no' or to turn the situation round with humour. Nursery rhymes and songs can help because they are playful (see p. 81). In practice, confrontational situations with violent resistance from the toddler and temper tantrums are common. In these cases, a decisive 'Stop now!' or 'No!' from the parents show the child that he can go so far and no further.

To summarize, you could say that within safe boundaries and rules, a toddler needs a great deal of space to discover himself and the world, but that he should not be allowed to decide on his own boundaries: these must be set by the parents. The more clearly they are imposed, the more easily the child will understand the reason. Conviction and a decisive approach by parents have a positive effect, while 'Yes, but ...' or 'Really you should ...' lack clarity. To make rules really clear, get into the habit of stating them firmly rather than asking for them. Many parents find this difficult because it sounds unfriendly and doesn't give the child much freedom. However, a question that's not really intended as a question and which cannot be answered with 'no' is confusing for a child. A friendly but clear statement, 'Right, now we'll take off your coat and then we'll put your boots on the mat,' is more honest and expresses your expectations more clearly for the child than, 'Would you like to take off your coat and put your boots on the mat?'

Punishments and rewards

With a punishment you can let the child know that his behaviour is bad and is not allowed. Rewards are a way of confirming desirable behaviour.

The aim of both these measures is to give the child an awareness of what is and what is not allowed, ultimately a sense of good and evil. This awareness hardly exists in children between the ages of one and four. A toddler is barely able to understand whether his own actions are good or not good, the relationship between cause and effect, or what another person feels. A toddler is just starting to discover that some things are interrelated. If you punish a child or reward him and then expect that he really understands why he's being punished or rewarded, i.e. appeal to his conscience, you are asking something of him which he is not yet capable of. Therefore punishments and rewards are not the basis for bringing up a toddler, but a means which can be used very sparingly to break down difficult behaviour, and in that case they can be very effective. When there are many strict punishments, the atmosphere in the home becomes tense and the child will eventually start to respond with fear or indifference.

This chapter clearly shows that a positive mood in the home, a good example and loving but consistent rules are the best way of encouraging the child to do what is expected of him. He will often need to be reminded, but in general does not need rewards. A toddler needs the confirmation and appreciation of the people around him in his everyday activities — by being stroked on the head or with an approving comment. Actual rewards or exaggerated praise can reduce the self-evident nature of the things the toddler is doing, and instead give the child an awareness that, 'If I do this, Mum will love me and I can have that.' However, rewards are still a better way of bringing up children than punishments, because a reward at least confirms that what the child is doing is right.

For special matters, such as toilet-training after a great deal of difficulty or to break down poor sleeping habits, tangible rewards in the form of something the child likes to have or do can be appropriate. For example, you can reward him with a shiny polished apple or a delicious pancake, or you can do something special together, like going to the playground or feeding the ducks. If you give too many rewards to get the child to do something, it will ultimately be the only way to motivate him.

It's important to be aware that by punishing a child he learns only what is not allowed. In order to learn what *is* allowed and how something *should* be done, you have to have the time and patience to show the child and practise together with him. He will have to practise many things again and again: brushing his feet, washing his hands, clearing up. If not enough attention is devoted to these things, it's unfair to punish the child when he doesn't do it well, even if it's only by reprimanding him. Once again, it's much more motivating to remain patient and to say something appreciative when the child performs a task well.

The two most frequently asked questions about punishment are whether you will damage the bond with your child by punishing him and whether you can crush the child's spirit. When you're punishing the child it's important that he does not feel rejected. To get it right, you should reject the child's behaviour, but not the child himself, and you will not have to damage the bond with your child. When a child disobeys, he feels his own strength and enjoys this sense of power. But to feel this strength it's not necessary for him to win; if he wins, he will have taken power into his own hands, which is a very unsafe feeling for a child. What a child needs is for you to provide a calm and decisive lead, and to avoid the situation resulting in a power struggle, because this will break both of you.

Many punishments can be prevented by taking a good look at what's really behind your child's actions when he's misbehaving. We often think the child is doing something naughty when he's simply engaging in exploratory behaviour. A child who grabs the biscuit tin on the table is not by definition being disobedient. Perhaps he's not intending to eat the biscuits at all, but likes the shiny tin or just wants to look at the biscuits in the tin or put them in a neat line.

Types of punishment

There are many different sorts of punishment, from a mild reprimand to corporal punishment. Appropriate punishments for a toddler include reprimanding him, removing him from an environment and separating him for a while, or to a lesser extent, punishing him by taking something away.

When you reprimand him, the words that you use are less important than the gravity of the way in which you do it. Telling a child off from a long way away, for example, shouting into the room from the kitchen, does not usually work. What works is going to the child, gently taking hold of his arm and looking at him, and then explaining in a few short sentences what is not allowed, but also what is allowed.

If a child won't stop resisting your requests, putting him in a different room can help. Remove the child calmly and decisively from the room and put him somewhere where he can do no harm. Tell him you will come back when he has calmed down. Some children are able to understand and judge when that moment will be, while others quickly make promises that they cannot make, such as, 'I'll never do it again.' In that case it's better to decide on the time yourself. Egg timers can be very useful because they clearly show the child when he can come back again. Finally, you can stroke the child on the head to show that everything is all right again.

Do not wait for the child to throw a tantrum before you remove him, because by that point the child will already have lost control altogether, he won't be in a position to learn, and it will no longer be safe to leave him on his own. If you find it difficult to intervene in this way, and always wait too long, hoping for the mood to become relaxed again, it may help to think about how often these situations calm down automatically and how often they result in a big scene. If the latter is more common, you could have prevented a great deal of irritation and conflict by intervening earlier. That's an important principle in bringing up children: it's better to deal with small problems than waiting for them to blow up into big problems.

A punishment that involves preventing a child from doing something he enjoys should only come into play when you can't make an alternative agreement; this starts to apply when toddlers reach nursery-school age. It's the type of punishment in which the 'offence' and the punishment must be very closely related. For example, a child of almost four plays in the garden in the morning, and it has been agreed that he's not allowed to go beyond the gate, but he breaks the rule and disappears. A logical punishment is that he must stay inside until lunchtime. But this punishment should not continue until four in the afternoon or into the next day. A small child lives above all in the present, and a long punishment is much too difficult for him to understand.

Biting and hitting

There can be all sorts of reasons why toddlers bite or hit out. It can be the result of a desire to explore, just to see what happens when you bite or hit someone else. Jealousy may play a role, or the child may opt for this behaviour because he cannot express what he wants.

This can often be prevented if you intervene in good time and distract the child. If he hits or bites he is doing something that's not allowed, whatever the reason behind it, and he must learn to stop this behaviour.

A small child experiences himself as the central point in everything and cannot yet feel the pain or sorrow of another person; the people around him have to teach him this awareness.

Therefore after the first reaction of, 'You can't do that, you're hurting your sister,' it's a good idea to focus the attention on the 'victim' and console her together with the toddler. If the biting or hitting doesn't stop, a consistent punishment, like being sent out of the room for a few minutes, will usually help to break down this behaviour. However, this measure must then be used every time the child bites or hits.

Punishing out of impotence

Punishments are by no means always well considered. In many cases the punishments are impulsive and based on anger or impotence. As a parent you may feel guilty in this situation, but the intention never to be so cross again is not very realistic. Take a good look at how your child responds to the punishment. In fact, some children feel relieved after this sort of scene because the air has been cleared and they feel strong in themselves again. Looking back, this kind of experience can encourage you to intervene earlier, and if necessary forcefully, next time, and teach you not to be afraid of imposing clear boundaries.

Other children (especially those who are very sensitive) may feel frightened or timid after a punishment. In that case the confrontation was probably too strong. After this kind of experience you may also decide to intervene earlier next time, but more calmly. However, this situation will certainly occur again and a sensitive child will have to learn to cope with it. The home is the best and safest place for this.

If you punish a child in a blind rage, you can be sure that it will not work, because rage and aggression never work when raising a child, particularly if you also hit the child. He will quite visibly respond with fear.

The problem with smacking is that the more often you do it, the lower the threshold the next time. Furthermore, the child will soon copy your example. Very occasionally rapping him on the fingers or smacking him softly on the bottom will not do any harm, but this habit never works well as a way of correcting the child.

When you punish a child in a rage or because you feel impotent, this is often accompanied by shouting. This is also something a child copies very quickly, which means that the mood becomes tense on both sides.

Threats do not work well, particularly for toddlers. Usually the threat is of a punishment or to withhold love. Threats which start, 'If … then …' often make the child feel frightened and he will obey in the first instance because of this. Afterwards these threats will challenge many children to find out whether the threat really is meant seriously, and you can soon become embroiled in a power struggle. If you do not carry out the threat, you also lose credibility and your child will take you less and less seriously.

Threats such as, 'If you do that, Dad won't love you any more,' have a very negative effect, because parental love is the most basic security a child has, and therefore should never be used by way of blackmail.

The toddler's three weapons

Not wanting to eat, not wanting to sleep and problems with toilet-training are sometimes referred to as the three weapons of the toddler. At first sight 'weapon' seems rather a strong word for a toddler, but the despair which parents can feel when their child will not eat or sleep can assume such proportions that the term 'weapon' seems justified from the parents' perspective. From the perspective of the child it is not an accurate term, because no child ultimately intends to lose the love of his parents with a fight.

Eating, sleeping and going to the toilet are all physical activities that a toddler can do by himself: he can eat by himself, sleep by himself and have a pee on the potty by himself. That's why it's so difficult when problems arise in one of these fields.

Earlier on we described one of the characteristics of the toddler as the ability to withdraw completely when you most want something from him (see p. 27). This applies particularly with regard to eating, sleeping and toilet-training. A child who regularly refuses to eat will not suddenly stop resisting and start to enjoy food when his parents stuff food into his mouth. And a toddler certainly will not stay dry by giving him a smack on the bottom, while the chance is very big that you'll find yourself in an endless power struggle with your child. To deal with these matters effectively you should firstly check whether there are any health problems. It's also useful to look at the way everyday life is going, because this may be able to shed some light on how to tackle the problem.

• What does the toddler's daily routine consist of? Is there sufficient variety in the day and is too much or too little asked of him?

• Does the child have enough freedom to move and does he go outside enough?

• What is he eating? Is it suitable for his age and does it look appealing?

• How is the parent's attention divided throughout the day?

• Are there enough clear boundaries or are there actually too many?

If one or more of these elements is missing or there isn't enough balance, you can start by tackling these issues.

4. Parents and Children

The family

These days there is enormous diversity in types of family. The family can refer to the immediate family but also to the extended family. The word 'family' is derived from the Latin *familia*, which means household. Whatever the family consists of, it is characteristic to live together in one house, to share the rooms in that house, and to spend (part of the) time together. The value of the family lies in the way in which adults relate to each other and to the children. In an ideal case, the family derives its strength from the mutual commitment, responsibility and safety, learning to share things together, to forgive each other and to support each other.

Because children copy the older members of the family in everything during the first years of their life, this means the adults in the family have an important responsibility. Looking after the relationship between the adults contributes to this.

Below we discuss three important qualities in a family.

'Home'

The term 'home' means the place where you live and the people you live with. It cannot be replaced and in principle there is only one home. Whatever the home is like, it only becomes a home when it's a safe place, where everyone feels they can be themselves and it's pleasant to be there.

This means that the space should not only be geared towards the children, but also towards the adults. It means that there are rules, not only for the children, but also for the adults. For example, for a parent the rule could be that she does not smoke indoors, and for the child that she is not allowed to touch the sound equipment.

One of the other special qualities of the home is that the objects in it often have a history. Previous generations may also have slept in the crib, the vase was grandmother's, the tricycle used to belong to the eldest child, the rag doll to the youngest child. These are all treasured things and they are therefore taken care of. In a home there is consequently a responsibility for each other, and also for the objects in the home.

Supportive relationship

A good relationship between the two parents and between the parents and children should be one of 'carrying' each other. This means that joy and sorrow, hope and disappointment are experienced together. You get up together, have breakfast together and the day is partly experienced together. Values and traditions are passed on. The bond that is formed in the family can grow, particularly during a child's first years when he's so dependent on her parents; the child becomes attached to the parents and feels safe in the home. For parents, the home is a safe point of departure for their other daily activities.

When parents divorce or families are combined, it can be a seriously testing time for the relationships between everyone involved. If parents have a secret, for example, about the origin of a child, this can also have a strong influence on the supportive relationship.

The responsibility of upbringing

A child depends on her parent(s) and very gradually develops to become independent. This dependence places the child in a very vulnerable position and puts an enormous responsibility on the parents.

You do not get any training for parenthood. Other people can, of course, make a contribution to the child's upbringing, but in the end it's the parents or principal guardian who has final responsibility. You are not aware of this responsibility all day long. If you were, you would probably struggle to bring up your child, weighed down by a paralysing fear. But just as you determine the direction of your own life, you also decide the direction of the lives of your children during the period in which you are bringing them up. You create the conditions in which everyone can develop. This means that neither the child nor the parent has a central place, but that the relationship of upbringing is central.

The more these three qualities — the creation of a home, maintaining a supportive relationship and taking responsibility for bringing up the children — have a self-evident place in the life of the parents, the more positive the influence will be on family life. Obviously every family has its own characteristics. In one family spontaneity may radiate in every direction, while another family may be much more formal by nature. A family with young children tends to be quite private and enclosed, while a family with adolescents fizzes with life and is much more worldly. The identity and the health of the family will influence the lives of both the children and adults.

Brothers and sisters

When a baby is born the relationships in the family change. If the baby is a second child, the first child is suddenly the oldest; when a third child is born, the second is no longer the youngest but falls in between, and so on. A great deal of professional literature focuses on the competition and rivalry between children; but the strong bonds between siblings less often take central place, while both these aspects are experienced in the everyday practice of family life.

In discussing this subject we started with the most common situation: the family with several children. For a family with, for example, foster children, a disabled child or twins, or for a family that is part of a larger community, the same starting points apply, but with individual emphases.

The family can be a safe place for a child to practise dealing with difficult things like jealousy, or where she can learn to share and wait. This aspect of the family is very often underrated, because the ideal image of the harmonious family tends to determine the norm. This is very much a matter of your own outlook — whether you think jealousy is difficult for your child and do everything you can to prevent those feelings, or whether you consider that it's part of life and you tackle the challenge together with your child so that she will learn to deal with it. It's not always possible or necessary to maintain harmony in

the family when working on social skills.

New brother or sister

The arrival of a baby in a family is by no means always easy for a toddler. You can only partly prepare a child for this event, but on the whole she will still be overwhelmed by all the changes.

In fact there can be all sorts of reactions. Sometimes a child responds to the newcomer by getting sick, which can be accompanied by a high fever. Sometimes a child responds to no longer being the youngest by making a leap forward in her new position, for example, by suddenly becoming toilet trained. Other children actually regress and display behaviour that they had previously left behind, for example, by starting bedwetting again or wanting to drink from a bottle. For these children it can be helpful if you don't make too many comments about being a 'big boy' or a 'big girl' already, and leave the child alone for a while. Usually this phase then passes automatically. In addition it can be helpful for the child if she can copy the things you do with the baby, for example, with a new doll.

Think carefully when arranging for visitors to come and see the new baby, as it requires all the attention of the parents and disrupts the normal rhythm of life. It helps a great deal if the visitors also take an interest in the older children in the family.

If children have been upset by all the changes, it's a good idea for their normal daily routine to be resumed as quickly as possible. A little bit of extra spoiling can also help, for example, going on an extra bike ride with Dad. Do not spoil the child by allowing her to do things that were not allowed before. This is very confusing for a toddler, particularly during a period that is already fraught with change.

When the baby starts to crawl, many things change again for the older children in the family. Suddenly nothing is safe any more, and in their eyes the sweet little baby has turned into some kind of monster that breaks everything. The playing area of the older children must be secured, for example, by regularly placing baby in the playpen. It can be helpful for older children to have their own place somewhere in the house, where they can keep their treasures safe and where they can play alone.

Brothers and sisters can also provide a great deal of support for each other. A child who wakes up afraid of the dark may feel so safe simply from the presence of a brother or sister sleeping with her that she goes back to sleep automatically. The big step to the playgroup or to infant school can also be taken confidently because there is already an older sister there. Conversely, an older child who is nervous at school may feel more confident at home with a younger brother or sister, where she can be little again and play with dolls.

Making a mess and having fun together happens from a very early age. It is often the first contact a toddler and a baby brother or sister will have together. During the baby and toddler period they will rarely really play together.

Arguments

There are quarrels in every family. Whether there is a lot of quarrelling or only a little depends on many different factors: problems with family relationships; one or more children who are difficult to get on with or who don't get on together well; a house that is too small. Issues such as these can all give rise to arguments. But this doesn't mean you are powerless in solving them.

First of all you can make sure, with imagination and humour, that many of the quarrels don't flare up into full-scale rows or tantrums, certainly with the youngest children. For example, you can distract a young child who is fighting about a toy and then playfully make her think of something else. By intervening briefly in the game and adding a new dimension, the subject of the argument is automatically forgotten.

In addition, it's enormously helpful if children are clear about what's allowed and what is not. For example, biting, hitting and throwing bricks or roughly taking away toys are not allowed, but defending your own things or keeping them safe is allowed. Obviously, children learn these rules by trial and error.

However, in a family many situations arise in which the rules about what is allowed and what is not are less clear. In these cases both the parents and the child must learn from the individual situations, which can gradually lead to new rules. In some cases, for example, if the children are simply squabbling over nothing, you don't have to intervene, while in other cases it will be necessary. Sometimes you have to protect one of the children, while another time you will have to intervene by setting an example. By talking about problems and looking together for solutions, children will learn that there are other ways to solve quarrels than by shouting or hitting. Anger plays a role in every quarrel, but so do sorrow and pain. It's only when both the anger and the sorrow have a place, for example, by discussing arguments with the children, that peace can be restored.

If you always take the side of one child and always blame the other, a pattern of quarrelling can be established: one child is more likely to start an argument because she will always be let off anyway, while the other child becomes indifferent because she always gets the blame. In the case of regular quarrelling, take a careful look at what's happening and listen carefully to what the children are telling you. Perhaps one child feels that he's not getting enough attention and has resorted to arguing to get your attention. If you look into the problem thoroughly and discuss it with your partner, you will often make new inroads and this can strengthen familial bonds.

The parents' relationship

In many cases when raising a family, the parents own relationship takes a back seat. Bringing up children is an immense task in itself. Work outside the home also requires a lot of energy, and in addition there are social commitments, maintaining the house, keeping up with finances, sport, etc.

The person who spends most time with the children can often find the toddler years a lonely period. Household chores take up a lot of time, looking after a toddler requires a lot of energy and the child does not yet go to school, sport or music lessons, which would give you some time for yourself. It's precisely during this period that you really need your partner. Always try to talk about what each of you has done that day or that week. If you are finding things difficult, try to work out for yourself, but also together, what the problem is. In order to do this, you need to be able to look at yourself without making any judgment. For example, admit that

you've had enough of your child when he's been naughty. It's only when you allow yourself to feel this emotion, and start looking into what you are finding difficult, that you can do anything about it. Usually you will then, above all, need to get your problems off your chest and be listened to and empathized with, rather than needing advice from the other person. Experience shows that women often identify problems before men and also talk about them sooner. Try to gain an insight into a problem by looking at it in practical, concrete terms. Stop panicking, 'It's so difficult, it's so draining,' and try to get to the bottom of what's making it so difficult, and then you can look for possible solutions (together).

Also include a regular time for rest in the week, both on your own and together. Try to spend time relaxing together and talking about something other than the children. Having dinner together, just the two of you, once the children are in bed, is a tried and tested remedy for parents who only manage to get together during the rush hours of family life — even if you only have time to get a takeaway.

However, you should also have the courage to discuss problems, even if that leads to arguing. If parents regularly quarrel in the presence of the children, as with other habits, it can set an example, and lead to tensions with the children and to further arguments. However, if you are able to resolve your problems through arguments, clear the air and become reconciled, you will set a positive example. Try to delay discussing disagreements that come up in the day until the children have gone to bed and you have time and space to really work them out.

While children are small, contact with other parents can be a great support. You can exchange experiences about bringing up children and about how to balance this with meeting your own needs. You can discuss particular issues with a group of parents, such as how to organize a day out with small children, punishments etc.

Childcare

There are all sorts of different types of childcare and you will have your own views about which are suitable for your child. Here are some things you may wish to take into account:

• You may choose to send your toddler to nursery or a playgroup, which will allow you to have a break and to meet other parents. If your child does not really play much and you don't have the creativity or the peace and space at home to expand on her play, a playgroup can be a solution. This can be particularly beneficial for only children, when a playgroup can

contribute enormously to the child's opportunities to play.

• Although childcare and playgroups for toddlers are becoming increasingly common, they are not essential for the development of social skills. Up to the age of four, the example you set yourself forms the main basis for the development of social skills, not playing in a larger group of children.

• If you opt for childcare because of work commitments, there are often difficult considerations to weigh up. On the one hand, you want to get back to work or you may have to financially, on the other hand, you have a responsibility to bring up your child. It's worth regularly weighing things up to see how the family is working and whether you are asking too much of yourself or the children, if everyone is getting what they need, whether there are enough times for relaxing and whether you spend enough time together (see also p. 30).

• A situation in which both parents work part time and are both at home for the children for part of the week can be the most attractive solution for many people, but in practice, it's hard to achieve. It would be wonderful if our society allowed more opportunities for this.

The most common forms of child-care are described below:

• A nursery provides options for looking after children for varying periods of time. You can choose different days of the week, mornings or afternoons, nights, weekends and during the school holidays. Groups may consist of children of the same age or of different ages. Sometimes there may also be an attempt to integrate children with physical or mental disabilities.

• A registered childminder usually looks after other people's children in their own home.

• A babysitter at home. This can be done through advertising or by asking someone you know, such as a relative or friend.

• There are playgroups for babies and toddlers, open to children from the age of two and a half and sometimes younger. Some parents organize toddler groups themselves at home.

Childcare usually stops at the age of four, when most children start primary or nursery school. Compulsory education starts at the age of five.

When you meet a childminder or a babysitter, take into account your first instincts on meeting them. If you have any doubts or do not completely trust that person, keep looking for someone else.

The period between eight months and two years is a very vulnerable period, particularly when a child spends more time in childcare than at home. At this age children often focus on their parents and can become very distressed when Mum or Dad suddenly disappears. If the child has become used to childcare before this vulnerable period, the response is usually less vehement. Every form of childcare has its own rules, procedures and financial considerations. It's important to consider your options thoroughly.

5. Caring for Toddlers

Diet

By the age of one a child has become familiar with a number of tastes, and his digestive system has learnt to cope with many foods other than his mother's milk. Nevertheless, it is important to carry on gently introducing the child to new tastes and foods over the next two years. During the toddler years the child learns to walk and think, and does not always have enough energy left to take on board and digest all sorts of new foods too. As he grows older, digestion, which can also be considered to be a learning process, becomes easier. It is important, and aids the development of a healthy digestive system, that meals take place in a relaxed and friendly environment and the food tastes good.

Eating patterns

During the toddler years, the child's diet will change as the hot food he eats becomes more substantial, and he can start to eat raw as well as cooked vegetables. The sense of taste develops gradually, initially with mainly sweet and sour foods, moving on to spicy, salty and some- times even bitter dishes. Important advice to remember with respect to a toddler's diet is that, as well as the development of the child's digestive system, the child's organs have to reach a certain maturity to be able to cope with the food we can eat as adults.

With regard to eating times, the child's eating pattern will usually have adapted to that of the adults after the first year of life. One dif- ference could be that the hot meal is eaten at midday, while the rest of the family has their hot meal in the evening. Digestion is easier during the afternoon, so if the child has any digestive problems it may help to structure their diet in that way.

There is an art to introducing a child into the regular routine of family meals round the dinner ta- ble while gradually developing their own dietary needs. Because of their healthy drive to imitate others, young children will mainly want to eat the same food as everyone else. You will have to use a little crea- tivity in finding ways to both meet this need, and in ensuring the tod- dler's dietary requirements are met. For example, you can start by giv- ing him his own food and then al- lowing him to try a little adult food and gradually increase the amount. When the child starts to eat full helpings of adult food, the family meal will have to be adapted to suit his digestive limitations.

In addition to the three main meals, a toddler also needs a few snacks in between. This is dealt with in more detail in the sections *Practical Advice.*

Over time, what the child likes and doesn't like will become increas- ingly clear. Every child has their own individual nature, which, to some extent, you can strengthen or counter with food.

Children who are on the plump side and who are not very active or excitable often have a preference for sweet, hot, creamy dishes. And to some extent these foods will rein- force this disposition. On the other hand, children who are thin and have an active and alert character often pre- fer savoury dishes and food that takes some chewing, such as raw vegeta- bles. In fact, this is the kind of food that stimulates them. Experience has shown that 'opposite' foods can help to make the child more balanced. Making dietary choices in the best interests of your child is one of the aspects of parenting, but never forget that eating should always be fun.

Food quality

Food is possibly even more impor- tant for a child than for an adult. Tests on animals have shown that if a young animal is raised on high quality foods, its health in adult life is guaranteed, even if the food available later on is of poorer quality. On the other hand, if the young animal is raised on food of poor quality, it can lead to poor health in adult life, which can no longer be improved with a good diet.

Obviously there are huge differences between different animals and human beings, but this can still provide important basic insights for us. The years of childhood also form the basis for later life and that's why the quality of a child's diet deserves particular attention.

On one hand, the quality of food is related to the composition of the product, but it also depends on its strength and vitality; the way in which a product has been grown has a big influence on this.

Using artificial fertilizers and artificial light results in a weaker plant; the natural resistance of a plant is reduced and pesticides are needed to protect the crop against disease. As a plant has the opportunity to grow at its own rate with organic manure, and is allowed to ripen fully, it becomes stronger and the natural resistance increases. In addition, the taste and preservation qualities improve.

In organic and biodynamic farming no artificial fertilizers or pesticides are used. And in biodynamic farming, extra measures are also taken to strengthen vitality. You could say that the products are given a more powerful 'identity.' These products can be identified by the term 'organic' in the product title. Look out for the Demeter label for biodynamic products.

The structure of food

For children a good diet must be a complete diet: it should have a healthy effect on a number of vital aspects of the child. Firstly, the senses are involved in eating: the food should look appetizing and invite the child to smell, taste and chew. The diet should also provide everything the child needs for good growth; they should feel comfortable after food, without becoming hyperactive or listless. Our preference is for a 'lacto-vegetarian' diet composed of cereals, dairy products, vegetables, fruit and possibly supplemented with nuts, seeds, lentils and pulses.

From an environmental perspective this diet is much less demanding than traditional meat and two veg. A number of further reasons why we prefer a lacto-vegetarian diet are summarized below.

Cereals and potatoes
Both cereals and potatoes consist mainly of carbohydrates. In principle, you could say that carbohydrates are created in the green parts of plants. The way in which a plant does this differs enormously for different species.

Cereals need light and heat to ripen, while the potato actually becomes poisonous if it's exposed to light (this happens when potatoes turn green). For humans, light and heat are vital factors for health; because of their strong relationship with light and heat cereals are very healthy foods for humans.

If you opt for a lacto-vegetarian diet, it's important that your child learns to eat different cereals, in the form of bread, porridge or muesli and in hot meals. We have seven different types of cereal: rice, barley, oats, wheat (and spelt), millet, rye and corn. They are often processed in ways that make the grains easier to digest (for example, bulgar wheat and couscous are processed grains of wheat). Every type of cereal has its own specific quality. For example, oats are a fatty and warm cereal, while barley is easily digestible and rich in silicon. Therefore variation is important. The next chapter describes which cereals you can give at which age.

We see the potato more as a vegetable to be eaten now and again, but not as the basis for a hot meal.

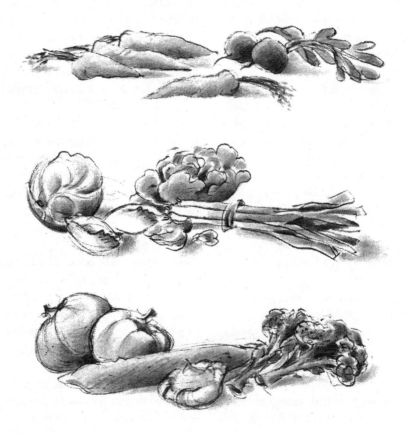

Vegetables

A plant consists of different parts: the roots; the stem and leaves; and the flowers, fruit and seeds. These different parts can be distinguished in vegetables. A balanced diet should consist of a combination of these three different parts of the plant.

In the table below the vegetables have been arranged according to the different parts of the plant and divided up in order of digestibility (from easily digestible plants to plants which are more difficult to digest).

All sorts of fruit, cereals, seeds and nuts can also be classified in the flower/fruit/seed section of the table below. They are not mentioned in this summary of vegetables, but of course play an important role in composing a balanced meal.

The vegetables marked with an * are rich in nitrates and are better not to include in the diet of small children more than twice a week. Buy these vegetables from organic or biodynamic sources wherever possible as this will affect the nitrate content, and always use them fresh. With the exception of beetroot, don't cook vegetables for very long, don't save the liquid they have been cooked in, and do not keep any leftovers.

Roots	Stem/leaves	Flower/fruit/seed
carrot	cauliflower	broccoli
parsnip	*fennel	pumpkin/squash
Jerusalem artichoke	*kohlrabi	peas
beetroot	*spinach	French beans
celeriac	*endive	runner beans
onion	chicory	courgette
	*pak choi	cucumber
	*Swiss chard	broad beans
	*celery	
	*lettuce (all types)	
	cabbage	
	sprouts	
	Savoy cabbage	
	curly kale	
	leek	

Eat the vegetables wherever possible when they are in season; this is better for the environment and for health, because vegetables grown in a heated greenhouse in general contain more nitrates.

Sources of protein

Foods rich in protein include dairy products, nuts, lentils, pulses (peas and beans), meat, fish, eggs and cereals. In a lacto-vegetarian diet, cereals serve as the staple foods, for example, brown bread with a beaker of milk or barley with grated cheese. The practical advice given in the next chapter for each age group describes in more detail what such a diet should consist of and how much a child should eat in a day. Do not feed the child too many protein-rich foods; the guideline is 300–500 ml ($^1/_3$ quart–$^1/_2$ quart) of milk or other dairy products per day. If the child is given too many proteins, this will put pressure on the organs. Quark and cheese are very concentrated and should be used sparingly.

Dairy products play an important role in providing protein in our diet. In addition to dairy products, meat and fish, nuts, eggs and pulses are also rich in protein.

We do not recommend meat, particularly during the first years of life, as it has the effect of 'waking' children up at an accelerated rate, preventing their own natural rate of development from coming into its own.

If you would prefer your child to eat meat, if possible opt for organic or biodynamic meat. In that case, you can guarantee the quality of food that the animal has been fed and be certain that it hasn't been treated with hormones or antibiotics. Fish is much more easily digestible than meat, but can often contain impurities, so organically cultivated fish is preferable.

Nuts can be finely ground and made into a paste, which will contribute to the nutritional value and taste of the meal.

Eggs are really only suitable for children over the age of two. The yolk is particularly difficult to digest.

Pulses are also rich in protein, but too difficult for a small child to digest. Lentils are an exception to this, as well as fresh legumes (peas, sugar snaps, small broad beans, French beans), which can be eaten as vegetables.

Soya is a well-known substitute for meat, for example, used in veggie burgers and sausages. We would not particularly recommend soya. It's processed in a huge number of products and barely retains its own identity. For a lacto-vegetarian diet, a range of sources of protein is available, all of which retain their own specific character; and this individual character is an important quality.

Fats

We need fats to promote the digestion of a meal. Good quality fats, such as milk, butter (in moderation) and cold-pressed oil stimulate the intestines, liver and gall bladder. It has also been shown that foods are metabolized much better if there is some fat available. The presence of some fat in the meal makes it more satisfying and provides a fuller taste. In addition, fats are important for carrying vitamins A, D and E, which are soluble in fat. These vitamins are found in dairy products (A and D) and in vegetable oils (E).

Milk should be processed as little as possible, particularly the milk of cows, which are given a great deal of room for movement and good food in organic and biodynamic farming. Therefore it's better not to use skimmed or homogenized milk (in which the fat globules are reduced). This is not done for milk with the Demeter label. Whole milk (with a daily maximum of 500 ml/ $^1/_2$ quart) is recommended in a lacto-vegetarian diet, and thinly spread butter can be used on bread.

Vegetable fats are found in nuts and nut pastes, in cold-pressed oils and seeds. Fats which are heated to a high temperature when frying foods are much more difficult to digest and therefore less suitable for small children.

Sugars

We recommend that sweet foods be avoided as much as possible in the diet. The child quickly becomes accustomed to sweet food and will want more and more.

Fruit is perfect for meeting the normal human desire to eat something sweet. Your child may also crave sweet foods like cake or pastries. Concentrated fruit juice and malted syrup or honey are suitable for meeting this craving.

White granular sugar can have a powerful effect on children: they can become hyperactive, aggressive, frightened or have difficulty sleeping. White refined sugar has the natural B vitamins that are still present in raw sugar removed (see the product information on p. 147), and it uses up the precious B vitamins that the child needs in other places in his body.

It's better not to use white refined sugar to stimulate metabolism in the body. These sugars influence blood sugar levels fairly directly. Many people experience this as a slight stimulant, but if too much is consumed it can seriously disrupt blood-sugar levels.

Sugars that are made by the body, for example, during the digestion of cereals, do not disrupt blood-sugar levels. They do not have the immediate stimulating effect of sugar, but do provide the energy a person needs in a balanced way. Because of this, cereals that require some digestion are much healthier than consuming refined sugar.

The child's body develops to be able to make its own sugars during the first years of life; cereals provide the opportunity for this.

We advise against the use of artificial sweeteners. They maintain the urge to eat sweet things, while they mislead the digestive system and set it on the wrong track.

Vitamins and minerals

In a varied diet — preferably an organic or biodynamic diet — with a broad range of fresh products, there should be no concerns about shortages of vitamins and minerals. However, the contribution of sunlight through the skin is also necessary to ensure sufficient vitamin D.

Food combinations

Some people recommend avoiding certain food combinations, for example, they recommend eating carbohydrates and proteins separately or suggest avoiding a combination of carbohydrates and fats. They maintain that digesting certain groups at the same time is difficult and puts pressure on metabolic processes. For example, they may suggest that fruit and yoghurt should not be combined.

In our opinion, it's true that protein and carbohydrates are easier to digest separately, but a healthy person should be able to assimilate combinations. Therefore a child should learn to digest combinations of foods. We do recommend separating foods sometimes, for example, if the child is ill or having digestive problems.

It's also said that a combination of fruit and dairy products should be avoided because it could have a negative influence on the assimilation of iron or vitamin C. It is a fact that acidic vitamin C, (for example, in fruit juice) promotes the assimilation of iron, while dairy products inhibit it, but this only has to be taken into consideration if there is a shortage of iron, not in the normal healthy situation. However, it's good for a child to get to know tastes of individual foods and therefore to also eat fruit separately.

Looking after the teeth

In general a child will have all his incisors by the age of one. Usually it takes a while before the first molars appear in the upper and lower jaw. The next teeth to appear are the canines. This happens just before or after his second birthday. The last of the baby molars then appear at the age of two and a half, and the first set of teeth are then complete with twenty teeth and molars.

Both the moment at which the first baby teeth appear and the moment when all the milk teeth are complete mark important developmental stages. When the first milk teeth appear, the oral cavity changes and the tongue also develops to produce the swallowing movement which is needed for more solid foods; in fact, this is a signal for letting go of the mother's breast, or where applicable, bottle feeding. The tongue is used in a more sensory way to taste, feel and perceive. The tongue is also responsible for the development of a harmonious shape in the line of teeth.

The milk teeth are complete during the stage when a child starts to use the word 'I.' At this stage he can also consciously swallow and rinse out his mouth and therefore start to really brush his teeth.

Defects in the teeth

Possible defects or developmental problems with the teeth become visible when all the baby teeth are complete. A few of these are briefly discussed below:

• There may be damage on the surface of the tooth enamel that looks like small stains or depressions. These originate during pregnancy, for example, as a result of the use of antibiotics. Intense emotional events during pregnancy can also affect the normal development of teeth. This is only manifested in the baby teeth, because the permanent teeth only develop after birth.

• A problem with the enamel does not necessarily mean that there is a weak or vulnerable area. Keeping the teeth clean is usually sufficient to prevent any adverse effects. In the case of doubt, the dentist can apply a protective layer.

• Deep grooves in the molars are very common these days. The layer of enamel is thin in these grooves or even partly missing, so that plaque can easily remain there and decay can develop. It's very easy to take preventative action by filling these grooves with a varnish.

• Baby teeth that point in the wrong direction are also very common. Normally, the arches of the milk teeth form a perfect semi-circle with small spaces between the individual teeth. The upper and lower teeth should fit together perfectly in a bite, with the upper teeth slightly overlapping the lower teeth.

• Teeth that grow in the wrong position can be the result of an incorrect swallowing action, for example, as a result of the use of a dummy. As the mouth is sucked into a vacuum during swallowing, this leads to significant forces, which can easily cause an 'open bite' where the jaws don't close together properly. Problems with swallowing action and an open bite are difficult to correct.

• Teeth growing in the wrong position appear to correspond with problems in motor development. If this is identified at an early stage, the parents, the child and health-care professionals all play an important role in correcting it.

Brushing teeth

From the time that the first milk teeth break through, it's possible to start getting the child used to brushing his teeth. Many children find it difficult to have their first teeth and molars brushed straightaway. Up to the age of two and a half to three years (until all the milk teeth have come through), the mouth is still subject to many reflexes. As a result children shut their mouth, push together their cheeks and lips or push the brush out of their mouth with the tongue.

If brushing the teeth is not successful, still check the teeth for plaque; this first appears between the gums and the teeth. Plaque can be identified as a soft white layer that is easy to remove with a piece of gauze or by brushing carefully.

A number of tips for brushing the teeth:

• A good introduction to brushing teeth is for the child to be there when the parents brush their teeth. The child can then join in and become familiar with the habits of brushing teeth in a fun, enjoyable way.

• It's a good idea to give the child his own brush from an early age, even if he only chews or sucks on it at first. Make sure that he doesn't start walking around with the brush in his mouth: serious injuries can result if he falls or bumps into something.

• When he tolerates the brush in his mouth, you can start to brush his teeth. It's best to use the scrubbing method: move the brush on the chewing surfaces of the molars from the front to the back and then tip the brush alternately inside and out, respectively to the tongue and towards the cheek. It's best to put the teeth together and brush horizontally.

• Use a small soft brush (special brush for toddlers) preferably made of nylon. As long as the child cannot rinse his mouth, it's advisable to use toothpaste very sparingly and at first brush only with water. It's very easy for children to swallow a lot of toothpaste, and the basic ingredients of toothpastes should not find their way into the stomach and intestines (Weleda toothpaste is an exception to this). Toothpaste encourages children who are just learning to brush their teeth to lick it from the brush rather than to brush carefully.

• Even if the child is able to rinse his mouth, it's advisable to use toothpaste sparingly: about as much as a small pea is sufficient.

• Make brushing the teeth part of a fixed ritual and this will avoid a lot of resistance.

• If the child wants to brush his teeth himself, it's advisable to brush them again afterwards yourself. This can be continued up to the age of about ten; brushing is a difficult motor movement, and the child does not always pay enough attention or have enough patience.

• Some children push the brush out of their mouths as a reflex so that the lower molars, particularly on the tongue side, are not cleaned properly. In that case, place the brush across the semicircle of teeth and brush from front to back. When you are brushing his teeth, make sure that the child is at the same eye level or place his head on your left arm so that it's easy to get to his teeth. One disadvantage of this is that it's easy for saliva to enter the throat, which encourages the swallowing reflex.

• For the upper jaw, it's recommended to also brush the back molars from the opposite side diagonally through the mouth because of the pattern of grooves.

Fluoride

The standard advice for toddlers is to brush with fluoride toothpaste twice a day from the time that the baby teeth and molars come through, in order to strengthen tooth enamel.

Fluoride is a very reactive element. The reaction to fluoride and the level of tolerance varies from one person to another. This is one of the reasons why we consider the standard advice to be one-sided, and we prefer to consider whether a child needs fluoride in their toothpaste on an individual basis.

Diet also plays an important role in ensuring the healthy development of teeth in a growing child. In addition to fluoride, a number of other elements are important, i.e. magnesium, phosphorous, calcium and silicon. There's a physiological balance between these elements. With a good diet, containing a variety of (wholemeal) cereals and green vegetables, it's possible to provide enough of all the building materials required. Non-carbonated mineral water contains the important minerals fluoride, magnesium and calcium for teeth.

If there is a real need to use fluoride toothpaste, for example, if the milk teeth are at a real risk of decay, you should brush the child's teeth with low fluoride toothpaste and make sure that nothing is swallowed. The presence of silicon, for example, in barley, oats and nuts, promotes the assimilation of fluoride in food.

Sugar

We have already discussed sugar in the section on diet, explaining that from the point of view of nutrition, the use of sugar is not necessary. Looking at the development of teeth, sugar is particularly undesirable. Sugar is converted into acids and plaque by bacteria that live in the mouth. Depending on the composition of the saliva, the effect of acids can take thirty to forty minutes. The repeated consumption of sugar or sugary drinks or sandwich fillings (including honey) and biscuits can therefore lead to a constant presence of acids in the mouth, which results in decay. Also remember that (concentrated) fruit juices have a high sugar concentration as well as many fruit acids. Really healthy drinks include (mineral) water, fruit/blossom tea, and fresh fruit and vegetable juices.

In order to meet the child's desire for sweet foods in a responsible way, set him limits with regard to the amount of sweet food he is allowed to eat each day. One clear rule could be: one sandwich with something sweet every day (after which the child should brush his teeth straightaway or have a piece of cheese to neutralize the acid) and one sweet or piece of chocolate a day.

The first cavity

Despite looking after teeth carefully, it's still possible for the enamel to be affected. In normal circumstances this rarely happens before the third year of life. With current modern materials and technology it's usually possible for the dentist to treat cavities without a drill, possibly with a temporary filling, to keep the trauma minimal.

Whether a child suffers from tooth decay differs enormously from child to child, aside from all the well-known causes and influences. Just as with childhood diseases, it depends on the child's individual vulnerability. The quality of saliva plays an important role. This is influenced by how a child feels in general, the amount of sensory impressions he has to process and the extent to which he is intellectually pressurized.

One form of decay that can occur at a very young age and sometimes immediately after the baby teeth come through is a consequence of bottle-feeding. This results from the habit of giving the child a bottle of milk — which may or may not be diluted with fruit juice or sweet tea — to keep him quiet. Similarly a dummy dipped in honey given to help the baby sleep has the same destructive effect. These sorts of bottles are particularly harmful at night because of the great reduction in the amount of saliva that is produced.

The first trip to the dentist

It is only from the age of two and a half to three years that a child is capable of understanding the purpose of having his teeth checked; in most cases he will be prepared to sit in the chair (maybe on his mother's lap) to have this done. It helps if the child has been familiarized with the room and the dentist in advance by taking him along when the parents' teeth are checked.

Childhood sexuality

It is important for a child to discover his own body from top to toe and this includes the genital organs. A child does not have the same awareness of sexuality as an adult. During childhood, the child focuses on himself and is involved in simple but essential physical experiences. The sexual nature that starts to focus on another person, a partner, only appears as a sign of biological maturity in puberty.

As parents we have most physical contact with children during the early stages of childhood: all the caring activities, carrying the child in your arms, sitting him on your lap, cuddles and pats on the head. Every child differs in his need for physical proximity and this need also changes as the child grows older. In many cases even bigger children still have a desire for physical contact and reveal it by wanting to playfight or tumble, but they also love to be cuddled or sit on someone's lap from time to time.

Experience shows that feelings of shame usually occur for the first time between the third and fourth year of life. Before that time most children like to crawl about without their nappy or walk about naked. It gives them a sense of freedom and an opportunity to discover themselves.

The more you can deal with nakedness in a natural way, the more the child can develop an innocent relationship without any pressures. It will help if it's perfectly normal for the parents, sisters and brothers to see each other naked, for example, in the bathroom.

When a child starts to experience a sense of shame, and this moment occurs for every child, this is an objective experience unrelated to his specific environment. Even a kiss from a favourite aunt or sitting on an uncle's lap can lead to a sense of embarrassment. If the child indicates this sense of shame, it should be respected and taken seriously.

Sometimes children stroke themselves before going to sleep or at other moments of the day. Girls like to seesaw on their tummy or hold a bear between their legs and boys play with their penis. This gives them a pleasant feeling. Sometimes children will do this at an inappropriate moment, for example, when you have visitors. In that case, protect your child; he doesn't yet know how other people see this. By picking your child up and cuddling him or distracting him you will help alleviate the situation for both of you.

Most children do not consciously see the difference between a man and a woman until the age of two. It's as though they look through the anatomical appearance and experience you above all as 'Dad' or 'Mum.' The point at which they do start making this distinction usually coincides with toilet-training (aged two to three): after all, boys pee differently from girls.

At the age of three to four children often start to play 'doctors and nurses.' This is a game of imitation, because by now they will have met the doctor a few times. The care and attention with which they listen to the lungs or tap on tummies in their game shows that they have experienced the care taken with the body, as well as nakedness. If you are allowed to join in the game as a parent, you can also devote attention to this element of care and respect with the naked body.

There are two essential rules in this game. The first is that no objects should be put into the genital organs or anus. The second is that if a child doesn't want to do something (for example, to be the patient), this should be respected by the other children. Perhaps his teddy bear could take his place.

If you think the game is becoming too one-sided, and focusing only on the genital organs, you can broaden it by providing bandages and slings so that broken arms and legs also become part of it.

At the same age, children start to find rude words funny. Usually this starts with words like 'poo' and 'wee,' but soon the use of language becomes wilder and is accompanied by lots of giggling. They pick these words up at playgroup, in the street or from an older brother or sister. It's difficult to find the right balance between paying too much or too little attention. Usually, ignoring it is sufficient, but exaggeration can also help, for example, by repeating the rude words together for five minutes.

Of course there's also the question of where babies come from. In contemporary sexual education, children are often given an honest adult answer, but this entails an element of dishonesty with regard to the child's capacity for understanding and feeling. A child cannot really grasp the technical details; he will feel better understood if the story is told through images. The old familiar image of the stork is not really so bad in this respect. It tells us that the stork comes flying from a distant country (cosmos, heaven), through enormous skies, flapping its wings to find a place for a nest (the child's house) and bring a child. Other parents talk about 'God' or 'heaven,' or talk about the little baby growing underneath the mother's heart. The image of a rainbow over which the new brother or sister has come can also be used.

It is self-evident that the amount of information and the way in which it is given mature as the child grows older. If you want to talk about spiritual aspects of life then you can only follow your own personal beliefs.

The way in which the child's feelings develop for other people will also depend on how you relate to other people as parents. If you have sincere and warm feelings and these are expressed, for example, in cuddles, the child will start to sense and experience how important other people can be in life.

The fact that children experience relationships differently from us is clear from their conversations. For example, they will ask one of Mum's friends whether 'she also has a father' and by this they mean whether she also has a 'husband.' Or sometimes you hear them say that they want to marry 'Dad.' Usually this is followed by, 'We will live in this house and Mum can come too, and brothers and sisters as well.' It's as though children understand 'marriage,' 'home' and 'living together' in a symbolic way.

We have said many positive things about the power of healthy physical contact but there are also dark sides, such as sexual abuse, which is more often committed by people in the child's immediate environment than by the infamous 'stranger.' With regard to the latter, it's good to teach your child at a young age to always ask you first before going along with someone, even if it's a friend. The child will then learn that he should never simply go off with someone and you will always know where your child is.

Toilet-training

Toilet-training is a natural and necessary stage in development. You could say that it's a milestone in the toddler years, partly because the child has to do it by himself. Parents can help by creating the right conditions and supporting the whole process in a positive way.

From about eighteen months, the child's nervous system is developed to the extent that he is, in principle, able to control the sphincter and the muscles of the bladder. Therefore

most children are toilet-trained between the ages of two and three, at least during the daytime.

The process of toilet-training starts with a vague awareness that something is happening lower down in the body. Then the child notices that something has happened and later becomes aware that something is going to happen. The last step is learning to postpone this urge until he has managed to get to the potty or the toilet. Some children learn this within a few days, while other children take weeks or even months to learn.

The more you want your child to be toilet-trained and impose this wish on your child, the greater the chance that he will resist you and not want to comply. This does not mean you shouldn't do anything for fear of resistance. It's also possible to build up a number of good habits in relation to toilet-training, creating an atmosphere in which the child is prepared to cooperate.

For example, make going to the potty or the toilet into a set habit without making too much fuss. Respond to the results in the potty, or to the lack of a result, in this vein. Toilet-training should be one of the most normal things in life, and the child should feel this in the reactions from the environment around him. Both exaggerated praise or rewards and anger or punishments are inappropriate, as is an exaggerated response to the smell of a dirty nappy.

Develop a good habit by cleaning dirty nappies straightaway. In this way, you are carrying out a 'toilet-training act' that could serve as an example.

There are different ways in which you can help to train your child. Everyone must find their own way; there's no one single good method.

When a child shows the first signs of noticing that something has happened down below — for example, by saying something about it, suddenly wanting to go on the potty or to the toilet, or by moving about and grabbing his trousers — it's always a good idea to respond to this immediately and make time for it. A number of children respond well to going straight to the potty or toilet.

If this is not the case, there are various possibilities:

• Wait until the next clear sign appears.

• Place the child on the potty or on the toilet at fixed times. Suitable times — when there is most likely to be a result — are after eating and after sleeping. Do not leave the child there too long (five minutes is long enough) or too often. Find out whether the child appreciates company during this toilet ritual or actually prefers to be left alone.

• Wait for good summer weather and then consistently do without a nappy for a period of, say, fourteen days. When they feel urine running down their legs, most children soon realize that this wet feeling is related to having a wee. A potty or the toilet should be close at hand for the next stage in this process: responding to the feeling of an imminent poo or wee. If this policy has not worked after two weeks, simply go back to nappies and try again a little while later.

Choose a good moment to start with the potty and leave off the nappy. Don't start just before a busy holiday, when there's a new brother or sister on the way or one has just been born.

It's possible that the use of paper nappies contributes to a delay in successful potty-training, because the layer in the nappy that keeps the child perfectly dry prevents him from feeling what's happening in the nappy. Cotton nappies are better than disposable nappies in this respect, and are also considerably better for the environment.

Potty or toilet?

A sturdy, stable potty can be a useful aid for toilet-training. If a potty appears in the home during their second year of life, the child can get used to it. Some children prefer to go to the toilet from the very start. It's not surprising: now that we have indoor toilets potties are no longer used anywhere else, whereas in the past, potties and bedpans were commonly used by adults.

A number of aids are available to help with starting to use the toilet: there are small seats so the child doesn't feel scared of falling in; a step can help the child to sit down by himself. For good hygiene, we recommended teaching little boys to pee sitting down. This makes using the toilet afterwards much more pleasant for girls.

A step back

Children who are already potty-trained can often regress when exciting things happen; a new brother or sister, going to stay in a strange place, moving house or Christmas festivities can all trigger this. Holding on to familiar habits and not making a fuss about little accidents usually works best. Illnesses or listlessness, cold feet or not having warm clothes can also be disruptive; fortunately these can all be remedied.

Constipation can lead to problems — if the child feels pain when going to the toilet. Sometimes you will find traces of faeces in their pants, which can be an indication that the intestines are too full and the child is keeping things in. Make sure that the child's diet does not promote constipation (no white bread, white rice, etc.), provide enough to drink, and if necessary add some extra orange juice, prunes or other laxative foodstuffs to the diet. Help the child to take the necessary time to go to the toilet properly, and if necessary contact your GP.

Don't put too much emphasis on cleanliness in everyday life; keeping things in can be related to thinking that poo and everything related to it is an exaggeratedly dirty thing. Sometimes it helps for the child to experience what fun it can be to get dirty, for example, by playing with sand and water.

Accidents usually happen when the novelty of being potty-trained has worn off and the child becomes so involved in a game that he fails to feel the signals. It often helps to remind the child from time to time or take him to the toilet and encourage him to go.

Children's clothes

How you choose to dress your child is, of course, a personal matter. The individual taste of the parent, whether you can make clothes yourself or not and financial considerations all play an important role in this. Below we have offered a number of viewpoints that may help to determine your choice. For us, the most important aspects are that you wrap the child up warm and use natural materials as much as possible.

Keeping warm

The body temperature of a baby is directly influenced by the amount of clothes or blankets he has around him. If there are too many, the baby becomes too warm and his temperature goes up, if there are not enough, the child cools down too much.

A toddler's body temperature no longer responds so directly to the influences of heat and cold from outside, and this is a sign that his homeostatis has become a little more independent. You no longer have to be quite as careful with a toddler as with a baby, but you still have to take into account the fact that a toddler cools down much more rapidly than an adult. Therefore, in general, the clothes have to be slightly warmer than those of an adult, particularly as a child still plays on the floor a lot at this age. In addition, it's a matter of making sure that you notice what the child needs as he does not yet have that awareness himself.

For the child's homeostasis it's important that the whole body feels nice and warm, down to the tips of the toes. If a child often has cold feet or sweats a lot, this should be discussed at your child health centre.

Choice of materials

The material with which a toddler's clothes are made is important in supporting their homeostasis. We advise choosing clothes made of natural materials, such as wool, silk or cotton, and pre-treated raw materials as little as possible. This is particularly important for clothes that are worn next to the skin. Woollen and silk underclothes are expensive but they last extremely well, particularly if the wool and silk are treated well by regularly airing the clothes and washing them by hand with a suitable, gentle detergent.

Advice and tips

Underclothes
We recommend giving the child a woollen vest to wear and only using cotton or silk underclothes on really hot days. These days, woollen underclothes are made of a soft knitted fabric, which doesn't itch as much as the home-knitted tops and vests of the past. Experience shows that children who have worn warm underclothes from infancy are able to feel whether they are hot or cold at an older age (from the age of seven) and are able to express this well. If a child of three is given a woollen vest for the first time, he initially feels much too warm. It takes a while before the child acquires a sense of the relative nuances of heat and cold. For example, in that case you can start by giving him a woollen vest to wear over his cotton vest or possibly giving him a silk vest.

In addition to a woollen vest, woollen pants worn over the nappy or ordinary underpants also help to keep the toddler's body warm. These sorts of woollen pants are ideal for toilet-training because they absorb the moisture well. After an accident, the material doesn't feel wringing wet, which is an advantage for children who have in principle already been toilet-trained, particularly in winter. For girls, wearing woollen pants is also recommended and this can usually prevent bladder infections.

At night
If a child is happy to wear the baby sleeping bag that he wore in the first year of life, he can continue to wear one as long as its length is constantly adapted. It will keep him beautifully warm even when he kicks off the blankets.

Outer garments
Outer garments serve predominantly to protect the child from cold and moisture. They should not be stiff or heavy as they need to allow the child to move freely.

Trousers generally fall down because the small child's figure is still very round and he doesn't yet have a waist (this only develops at the age of five or six). Usually you see the vest and T-shirt outside the trousers. Trousers with elastic or braces are a good solution. Wide dungarees or romper suits also provide sufficient warmth and freedom of movement.

A cardigan can be useful and practical to have at hand. Furthermore, a child can take it off himself when necessary from a young age.

Thin woollen or cotton sweaters are comfortable to wear, but many children feel uncomfortable because they can be difficult to pull over the head. Sometimes this can be solved by undoing a seam at the neck and securing it with a button and a loop.

Party clothes

Festive clothes can add an extra dimension to a party. It's wonderful for a child to put on a new dress or pair of trousers on the morning of a party day after seeing it hanging in wait in the wardrobe. Parties create a sense of anticipation. Everything is a bit different. The food, the people and the clothes go with this. Children can enjoy this intensely and these are often precious memories later on.

Special clothes are often used for special jobs; there's good reason why the farmer, the baker, the conductor, the postman, the cheesemonger and the mechanic all look 'different.'

At an age when the child is overwhelmed by the variety of different activities and then copies them, work clothes are particularly useful. In addition, it often helps to create order. In the kitchen — apron on. When the work is finished — apron off.

Outside

In winter a ski-suit can be very useful, as well as a warm coat. Waterproof trousers with braces, worn over ordinary trousers, are ideal when the grass is still damp or the sand in the sandpit is wet. In winter a hat is essential, and in summer a cap or a hat with a flap keeps the sun off the child's face. This is particularly important on the beach.

If you carry your child on a bicycle, he can often feel the wind more than you think. While you're peddling, your child is sitting still. Therefore a basketwork seat on the back of a bicycle is recommended so that the child is shielded from the wind.

Buying clothes

Buying clothes without children is usually more fun than with them. This gives you all the time you need to have a proper look, and your attention is not distracted while you are trying to decide what will suit your child. It is only appropriate for children to choose something themselves from the enormous range of clothes available at a much later stage. The range of clothes in shops tends to closely follow the fashions for adults, while small children still live in a completely different world. As Annie M.G. Schmidt remarked, 'That's the country where the grown-ups live … you don't have to go there yet.'

If you enjoy it, you can, of course, make clothes yourself.

Shoes

Shoes have a fascinating effect on small children. New shoes are constantly admired, and many boys and girls like to walk away in mother's high-heeled shoes or father's work shoes or clogs.

When buying shoes it's very important to take into consideration the following points:

• Only buy real shoes for the child when he can walk well. For the first attempts at walking, shoes are a hindrance rather than a help.

• Feet should be able to move without restriction and bend and stretch well. When the child stands up and walks, he uses his toes to keep balance, therefore the shoes should be made of flexible, supple leather.

• Have both feet measured for length and width (they should be re-measured every three months), so that both the length and width sizes are right. There should be enough room around the toes.

• If possible buy shoes without a preformed sole so that the foot can develop freely in its own way.

• Shoes with laces retain their shape better than shoes with Velcro.

For the development of the foot muscles, it's recommended that children alternate between walking in shoes, clogs, sandals, slippers and bare feet. Particularly in beautiful weather when the grass, sand or gravel have been warmed up by the sun, the child has every opportunity to walk around in bare feet.

Children in colder climates mainly have to wear closed shoes. Restrict wearing boots to wet weather because the feet are not able to breathe in boots. In summer, sandals with a closed heel and a broad strap or crossed straps at the front are preferable to plimsolls, which can fit poorly. Furthermore, any plimsolls other than cotton ones are too cold to wear in winter and unsuitable for summer wear as they restrict the flow of air.

Socks and slippers

Warm woollen socks, tights and slippers keep the child's feet, legs and thighs beautifully warm. A sock should be big enough, both in length and width, for the toes to have sufficient room. The edges should not pinch. Stretch cotton socks a little before putting them on.

In most families it's a good habit for the children to take off their shoes or boots when they come home. This means that the muscles of the feet are also exercised indoors. The child could wear socks with integrated soles, small clogs, woollen socks with a leather sole underneath or slippers. The sole should be hard enough to ensure that he does not slip.

Play and toys

A child often beams with pleasure when he's playing. When you look closely at a toddler engrossed in games you can see, on the one hand, the serious way in which he is involved, and on the other, the absence of any clear goal. The child is not playing to learn or because he wants to develop, but because he likes to play. That is the reality of the child, and it's on that basis that we want to look at a number of aspects of his play.

Playing is necessary for healthy development. While he's playing, the child has all sorts of experiences and in this way learns about life and his culture. Up to primary school age, play, work and learning coincide completely in one intensive experience. The child's physical control, sensory development, language and cognitive development, and social intercourse are practised while playing, working and learning. What do we see when we look at a child who looks as though he's enjoying playing? He's completely engrossed in the game. His consciousness has a dreamy quality. The child perceives everything, accepts everything for what it is and doesn't observe things in the way we do.

It looks as though the child is endlessly active. He surrenders to his play without any reservations. The more the child is engrossed in his play, the more he seems to be outside time.

Children experience time and space in different ways, both in the home and outdoors. Adults often remember this from their own childhood: the garden in our parental home seemed so big, but when you see it again, you're surprised at how small it actually is.

The awareness that a toddler is engaged in his play above all in a dreamy way, and that he experiences time and space very differently from us, can help you to create the right conditions for play.

Conditions

Everything the child experiences as pressure on time disrupts his creative play. It's upsetting for a child if he's removed from his play for a trifling matter, and it can help to tell him in advance what's going to happen.

In general, homes are larger now than they used to be, and there are often fewer people living in the house. Although many toddlers and infants have their own room, they rarely play there because they want to play where the adult is. It's when they go to primary school that children gradually find their own room attractive, but only when they are not banished there.

The living room should be furnished in such a way that both children and adults have the chance to express their creativity there. A comfortable living room in which a child can move about freely is experienced as being much larger than a room where nothing is allowed. After all, you can do many things with the sofa apart from just sitting on it: you can hide underneath or behind it; sometimes it suddenly turns into a boat and you can sail away in it with your favourite doll, and you're the captain; when you're ill it may become your bed; and with the loose covers you could make a house underneath the dining room table.

For a child it's wonderful if the garden is organized in such a way that he can play hide and seek and experiment with sand and water to his heart's content. A large tree trunk can be an exciting thing in the garden. A few pieces of wood can be used to walk the plank, as a springboard or to make a hut. Even a washing rack with some clothes can be turned into a little hut. Rocks, beautiful stones from a holiday and wonderful roots can turn the garden into a play paradise.

If you don't have a garden but you have a balcony, it can also be organized in such a way that a child can really play there.

There are many things to experience outside the garden. Children like to explore fields, along ditches, in meadows and woods.

The rain, the wind and sunshine, and in the evening the stars, are all new experiences. Ideally a child should go outside every day and make his own discoveries there.

Developments in play

Infants are mainly engaged in discovering their own bodies and the people around them. For the toddler, the world is already much larger than it was before. A one or two-year-old goes on voyages of discovery. Everything in the home will be examined, from the table leg, to the wastepaper basket and the sieve in a kitchen, to the socks in a drawer. A drawer that can open and shut, or the doors of a storage cupboard are experienced by the child as something which conceals a hidden thing, i.e. a secret. There are so many things in the world which are seen by adults only in terms of practicality, but which provide the child with many rich experiences.

As he plays, the child learns to understand natural laws such as gravity. When he throws something from the high chair, the child looks at it and wants to try it again. In this way he discovers that a ball is round and will always roll, unlike a square brick. He will practise with these things until he has built up an inner certainty about them. This gives him a sense of confidence that he can build on.

Getting to know sand and water is also part of this voyage of discovery. You can sit in sand, you can put it in your mouth and you can play with it. You can play pat-a-cake with moist sand, while dry sand simply slips out of your hand. Water makes you wet, you can pour it out and the drops fall from your fingers.

In addition to discovering the world in and around the house himself, the child also likes to join in the things adults are doing, preferably at the same time, in the same place and with the same things. Of course, this is disruptive for you as you can do the household chores much more quickly on your own, but nevertheless it's worth involving your child whenever possible in household tasks. He'll enjoy joining in with hanging out the washing, sweeping, cleaning windows, polishing shoes, cooking, baking, working in the garden, and so on.

At the age of three, the child's play changes, although it may at first sight still look the same. However, if you look closely, you'll see the child start to take hold of a cloth in his own play corner and start dusting shelves. He is pretending to be the Dad or Mum and the cloth serves as the duster; he is pretending that the play house is a real house and he will talk about this. Sometimes you can hear the child using words that you have used yourself when you're dusting. The child could already do the dusting with intense energy and seriousness before the age of three, but at that stage he was unconsciously copying your actions, while from the age of three to five the child actually imagines being someone else, using the power of his own imagination. It is only then that the child will start to feel the need for objects to help him to express his imagined role (working clothes, clogs, cloths). At this stage the child is ready for grown-up things in miniature, such as little pans for a child's cooker, a child's broom, a small iron, a train with rails, and so on.

Toys

During the first to third year, children are happy to play with anything found in the home and by no means always have a preference for 'real' toys. Furthermore, children often use toys in a very different way than you might imagine.

Any toys, including utensils which they pick up and play with in the house, must be solid, not splinter and not be treated with toxic paints, and they should not have any small breakable parts.

Wooden toys are usually preferable because they are durable, which allows the child to really become attached to them because they don't get broken and have to be discarded after a short while. If a wooden toy has to be repaired, the child will usually find this very interesting and will enjoy watching and helping.

The disadvantage of synthetic toys is that they are very lightweight, and feel much lighter proportionally than the object they imitate, for example, a heavy lorry. They are often brightly coloured, which can in a sense keep the child's eyes fixed on only one element of the toy, the bright colour. Furthermore, synthetic materials have a big impact on the environment and the bright colours sometimes contain the harmful element cadmium, which is released when the waste materials are incinerated.

In the first few years, the less 'finished' toys are, the more the child can 'build' on them with his own creative imagination. A block of wood can become a car for a child, and a little later it becomes part of a tower or a table for an elf, depending on what the child is doing at that moment. As he is playing, his imagination becomes more and more powerful, until he becomes completely absorbed in imaginative

play from the age of three. The child can become the mother, the father, conductor or the doctor in his game, and dolls, cooking utensils, conductor's accessories or a doctor's case will be very welcome.

If a child finds it difficult to play, it's a good idea to look critically at the number and type of toys he has. Too many toys can be paralyzing. When you're in the supermarket and you have a choice of ten different sorts of cream for your coffee, you often find it difficult to choose one. The child will often start playing again when some of the toys have been removed and he is given the opportunity and space to play with things in the house.

If children only have toys that have to be played with in the way that's intended, they often tire of them very quickly and are constantly looking for new stimuli. This can make a child restless and dissatisfied. Take a careful look at his toys and if necessary put some away. If difficulties in play remain a source of concern, discuss them at your child health centre.

Finally, playing and tidying-up go hand in hand. At the end of the day, and possibly also before the afternoon nap, it's a good habit to put everything back together, everything in its own place: 'The bricks are going to have a rest, just like you are.' A toy box in which everything disappears into one big heap does not encourage the child to want to play the next day. Shelves in a cupboard with different baskets or boxes for the bricks, blocks and other toys work better. Older toddlers sometimes build structures or large railway tracks that they work on for days, becoming engrossed in the game. Obviously, it's good to encourage this by allowing such structures to remain standing for a while.

Children and dolls

For a child a doll can be a faithful friend who supports him through thick and thin. The child and the doll form a unit, particularly if the doll has also taken on the child's smell. It is as though the doll has become a part of the child with which he can talk, have fun and share his sorrows. Sometimes the doll acts as the scapegoat for something the child has done himself. In this way the child is able to distance himself from his own actions and feel liberated from feelings that he cannot grasp yet. At other times he will cuddle the doll and snuggle up with it. The doll can be a confidant and dearly loved friend for several years to come. It's particularly during difficult or exciting situations, for example, when the child is left with a baby-sitter, when he is admitted to hospital or during a divorce, that the doll can provide enormous consolation; it can give children a sense of security when their trust is tested. In this way, the doll accompanies the child on his way through the years of childhood. Give the child the space to decide for himself when he is ready to leave the doll behind, even if this may sometimes take a very long time.

Obviously it's not only a doll to which a child can become attached. It can also be a comforter, a sleeve of a pair of pyjamas that has been sucked on, a knitted gnome or a teddy bear, rabbit or lamb. Usually a child only chooses one cuddly toy to be a faithful companion, and so he doesn't need to be given many. It's up to the parents to choose what sort of cuddly toy the child is given. If it's a doll, you give the child a 'human' companion, which is a different thing from having an animal as a friend.

It's self-evident that both boys and girls feel the need for this faithful companion. It's only at a later stage that boys and girls differ in the way that they look after their 'child.'

A doll who becomes a faithful companion for life can be very simple, such as a rag doll. The softness of the material and the woollen stuffing are an invitation for a cuddle. Gradually the doll acquires its own smell. A rag doll often has a simple face, which means that there's room for the child's imagination to attribute any expression to the doll, depending on the mood of the game at the time.

There are books that can show you step by step how to make such a doll, from a very simple box doll to dolls with hair and limbs (see bibliography p. 149). In addition, courses on doll-making are available and, of course, you can buy rag dolls in a variety of shops.

Drawing, painting and modelling

Most children love to draw, paint and play with modelling wax. The child will become completely engrossed in this, just as he is when he's playing, and here, too, the important thing is the fun of doing it and not so much the result. In this sense, you don't have to teach children anything at this age — they do it themselves automatically. You simply have to provide the right materials, take some good precautionary measures and stay nearby so that the child can 'get to work' in peace and quiet. Constantly giving instructions or asking what the child has created will have an inhibiting effect on him and can make him feel uncertain. He wants to discover things for himself.

Drawing

The first attempts at drawing for a one-year-old toddler are above all an exercise in holding a crayon. The child can barely see what he's doing, but it gives him pleasure to carry out the movements and he enjoys the surprising fact that something appears on the paper. These are 'scribbles.'

Gradually the child will also start to tell stories that are reflected on paper. We can see little of what is represented. Above all, we see the round and straight scribbles on paper. Sometimes there's a tight tangle of scribbling. Usually the upper body of the child moves about while he is drawing; he becomes completely engrossed in his movements and can hardly stop. While he's drawing, the drawing moves in every direction, there's no top or bottom, no left or right.

At about the age of three, when the child starts to refer to himself with the word 'I,' he will start to draw circles, suns, round patterns or other enclosed shapes. It requires great concentration to complete these circles. Sometimes the child confirms the growing sense of self by placing a dot in the middle of the enclosed form.

Gradually the child is better able to direct his movements on paper and the drawings make a less chaotic impression. He tries things out again and again, creating drawings full of drops and dots and flowers.

At about the age of four, the first signs of a stick figure with a head and legs, as well as circles, will emerge — this is the first drawing of the human figure. The child's world is gradually becoming larger and he is strongly focused on this outside world. Sometimes you can see this in the 'antennae' that he draws on the hands and feet. There are all sorts of suns on the paper and the rays of the sun radiate in every direction. There is a top and a bottom, a left and a right.

Children also often draw houses. Initially they are represented by an

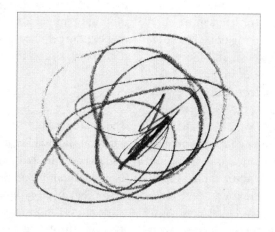

arch or a circle, but at about the age of four, you will see signs of a rectangle. Later, at about the age of five, the child may draw a triangle on the house to represent the roof. In this way he starts to draw increasingly recognizable things in his environment. By the age of seven the child is drawing whole people with a torso, head, hands and feet.

Recognizable drawings are no more valuable than the first scribbles a child puts down on paper. By drawing, the child shows what is happening inside him and in this way every drawing is a sort of open book.

Until the age of three, drawings are mainly coloured by all the changes that are taking place in the toddler's body, in terms of physical development and illnesses. After that, the things the child experiences, what is going on inside him and the impressions things make are also reflected in the drawings. All sorts of different stories are told in the drawings because nothing is yet fixed. What is a forest one minute can become the fence around granny's garden the next, or Dad's table.

Painting

Children love colour and painting allows them to make even more use of colour than drawing, where lines and shapes are also important. When they paint with blue paint they feel blue; the inner and outer worlds are not yet very separate, and children can experience the quality of the colour in a very physical way.

As the child grows older the experience of colour changes and is partly replaced by a stronger sense of shape. The child recognizes things and understands more about the world. Therefore he sees the shape and use of an object first, and no longer mainly the colour.

A two or three-year-old can already use water, paints and brushes. Don't give the child too many colours at the same time at this stage. Often one colour is enough. If he starts to use several colours together it soon turns into a brown soup on paper.

Playing with modelling wax

Children like to touch everything, not only with the tips of their fingers, but preferably with their whole hand. They also like to do something with the things they touch; they fiddle with everything, they look to see whether something can be squashed or whether they can remove the colour. They want to leave their stamp on everything, recreate things, as it were. This is the creative impulse in children. Usually this is a difficult aspect to deal with and sometimes there is nothing you can say but, 'Hands off!'

Fortunately, when playing with modelling wax, kneading dough or making sand patties, children can touch as much as they like. Playing with sand and beeswax can often have a calming effect in children.

Materials

When painting and drawing, don't use paper that's too thin, as the child will easily go through it with his brush and the paper will crease when he's drawing.

For drawing, painting and playing with modelling wax we recommend materials based on beeswax and plant dyes.

Coloured beeswax crayons are great for drawing. They can be used to make beautiful blocks of colour. When using coloured pencils, children often draw in a very detailed and fussy way, which can take away the child's pleasure because he's not yet able to draw in such detail.

Watercolour paints are great for painting and you can use them to paint 'wet on wet.' If they are diluted and painted on to damp paper the child can make beautiful blocks of colour with his brush, without creating any hard edges.

For modelling we recommend using coloured slices of modelling beeswax. Clay is less suitable because it remains very cold when kneaded and cracks very easily when it dries. Beeswax is hard to begin with, but by kneading it for a while in your hands, it becomes warmer and you can make shapes with it. When the work is finished, the beeswax turns hard and remains in the shape it was kneaded into. When the child has finished with whatever he's made, the wax can be reused.

Kneading and shaping dough is also a popular activity, particularly if you can eat it when the dough has been in the oven.

Nursery rhymes and songs

Every child has a sense of music, or of the musical aspect of the sounds he hears. You will notice this in the way in which a baby listens to your voice, and the way in which he makes noises himself: it's as though he's tasting the sounds. The baby's hearing is also extremely sensitive. He hears sounds much better — and therefore often earlier — than adults. He assimilates the sounds in an uninhibited way without the immediate associations we have. This lack of inhibition is still very much present during the toddler years, but at the same time understanding gradually develops. By singing songs or repeating nursery rhymes, you connect with the uninhibited and musical capacity of the child; by reading books you connect with his emerging understanding.

The first time parents sing to a child in their arms or on their lap, they often feel embarrassed because they think, 'I can't sing.' It's true that many adults have forgotten how to sing, certainly the very simple childhood songs that babies and toddlers enjoy. Fortunately, young children are not so critical of their parents' singing, so just do it! Children love being sung to and it certainly calms them down when they go to sleep.

When you recite nursery rhymes, it's not important for the child to understand exactly what the words mean, and often they don't make much sense. The child hears the melody in the poetry and hears the alternating tones of the reassuring lines followed by the slightly more threatening lines, and enjoys this. He loves hearing the same nursery rhyme over and over again. With the first sentence you'll often see the enthusiastic recognition of, 'Here it comes again!'

The rhythm in songs and nursery rhymes also appeals to children. They love being rocked to the rhythm or moving along with the rhythm themselves. Most nursery rhymes are very suitable for this: children can often make movements to nursery rhymes such as 'Incy wincy spider' and 'Round and round the garden' even before they can speak.

At about the age of three, children achieve a kind of high point in their sensitivity to rhythm. They often ask you to come and sit down on the ground with them in order to do 'The wheels on the bus go round and round' or they climb on your lap for 'Ride a cock horse.' They like to swing and be bounced up and down, and they appreciate fixed habits.

Nursery rhymes and songs can also encourage children to carry out daily tasks. While the order, 'Brush your teeth!' may lead to resistance, and a discussion about the importance of clean teeth certainly won't

achieve anything, children may be sensitive to a nursery rhyme about this. There are many traditional, as well as new, nursery rhymes about the daily life of a toddler (see bibliography p. 149), nursery rhymes to accompany a meal or going to sleep, for things that hurt or for when it rains, or just for repeating again and again. Having some of these nursery rhymes at hand will give your child a great deal of enjoyment and will enable you to change difficult situations with your child, or even to pre-empt them.

Sometimes it's fun to make music for your child, for example, when he's going to sleep or when you're telling a story. If you don't play an instrument, there are a number of simple instruments on which you can easily play music, even if you can't read music, including the recorder, a little harp or a xylophone. Some of these instruments are tuned in the pentatonic mode; playing and improvising in this mode always sounds beautiful, and experience has shown that children like to listen and pay attention.

When your child listens to a tape or a CD this has a very different effect from singing and making music yourself. Admittedly this music can also meet your child's musical needs, but often the child will stop really listening and it will become background music. If this happens you are merely adding to the general background noise, to which the child is already overly exposed. There are increasing warnings about the danger to children who constantly have background music around them; they learn to listen less effectively as they become less sensitive to the fine nuances of sounds. To some extent the increase in deafness in children could be related to this.

Telling stories and reading to children

One way in which you can feel really close to your child is to read to him, or tell him a story. If you can find a quiet time for this, it will be a moment that you will both enjoy. These moments of warmth and companionship are worth gold in bonding with a difficult child or a child who craves attention in a busy family.

The stories you tell or read to the child should be suitable for his age. During the baby years and the first toddler years, stories and books barely play a role. At that age the child particularly likes to listen to songs and rhythmic nursery rhymes.

When a child starts to speak and to name the things around him, the content of the language assumes more of a place in the child's world, as well as the musical and rhythmic aspects, and you can start telling stories and looking at books together. Children like it when you look at the same book or tell them the same story again and again. This need for repetition continues throughout the toddler years.

There's a difference between telling stories and reading to a child. When you tell a story, the child listens and uses his own imagination to 'dress up' the story. Children will endlessly enjoy stories you have made up. It's best if the characters in the story are recognizable and the events of the story vary. You can take inspiration for stories from looking carefully and listening to what your child experiences during the day. A toddler doesn't need much variation. The same characters, the same sentences and intonations will form a structure in which events can be amended to contain surprises, which make the stories exciting. Every time the child will recognize the excitement coming ... and the story may even get quite frightening ... but it will end happily ever after, and he'll breathe a sigh of relief, even after the hundredth telling.

When you read to a child, you use a book. Initially this may be a board book without any text and you will tell your own story. The pictures often show people and animals or objects and events. For the first time in a child's life there is a combined perception of a picture and words. It's only by repeating the same word or the same story alongside a picture that the child learns that certain words or sentences belong with certain pictures. This is a step forward in his development.

This is followed by a picture book, which has many pictures but little text. Finally, a child of about four will reach the stage where he can remember the thread of the story when a real book is read to him.

The illustrations in a book should be suitable for the child's age. In the bibliography we mention a number of (picture) books in which the illustrations suit the rich and imaginative world of the child (see biobliography p. 149).

Telling stories and reading to the child puts him in contact with language. Good language development is important for cognitive development, and by telling stories and reading to the child, you contribute to this development. The older the toddler, the richer the language you can use. You can help the child to 'taste' words that are not often used in everyday language, helping him to learn the nuances of language so that he can gradually use richer language himself.

Listening to stories on CD does not really compare with having a book read to you. You do not see the person who is reading, let alone be able to sit on their lap. You do not see the mimicry, and the intonation is the same each time.

For some children it's more important to be read to than for others. For children who are very busy and active, reading a book can encourage them to learn to listen quietly. But for children who want to understand everything, who constantly want to talk to you and ask 'Why?', reading a lot may reinforce this nature; perhaps you should look for other things to do together, such as craftwork, playing with modelling wax, working in the garden or going to the woods.

The child and the seasons

During the years of childhood, the child starts to recognize more and more of the world around him and the things that happen in it. Learning about the seasons is one of these things. Initially the child recognizes the everyday habits of the family; we have already mentioned that it's a great support for the child to have a daily routine. He will also start to recognize different days of the week, especially if these days involve special events, such as a treat for dinner on Sunday, going to the market on Wednesday, helping to put the dustbin outside on Thursday, etc.

If the family around him is aware of the changing seasons, they will also start to play a role in the young child's life. Firstly, from direct experience: in summer you walk on the grass with bare feet, you can play with water outside and it's still light when you go to bed; in the autumn there are storms and it rains, you have to wear a warm coat and put on a hat, and you can find chestnuts and acorns; in winter the world is sometimes suddenly white with snow, birds come to eat the food that you put out and it gets dark very early; in spring you see little ducklings and lambs, new leaves and flowers appear everywhere, and you can play in the sandpit again.

All these experiences can also be given a special place in the home by placing all the seasonal treasures found outside on a special nature or seasonal table, and making sure it gets updated and looks attractive throughout the year.

The child will also experience the cycle of the seasons through his food. By using the products that naturally grow during a particular season of the year, the child will become physically familiar with the different seasons.

Finally, there are many annually recurring festivals that familiarize the child with the seasons in an intense way. For many adults, memories of Christmas, for example, are the best memories of their youth.

The way in which you celebrate these festivals with children depends on your own attitude towards them. Annual festivals usually have a religious aspect and a natural aspect. For example, at Christmas you celebrate the birth of Christ, but you also celebrate the return of light after all the months in which the days became shorter. The elements of annual festivals that relate to nature have been celebrated since time immemorial, and the religious elements come from different religions.

The aspects of the annual festivals that relate to nature always appeal to children. By celebrating these festivals the child can develop a sense of respect for nature and its produce. In terms of the religious aspects, that is wholly dependent on your own religious views.

The bibliography suggests books that can be an inspiration for cel-

ebrating the many well-known and less well-known festivals. Festivals such as that of St Michael, when all the riches of summer are gathered together, and of St Martin, when the child brings light into the dark night with his little lamp, are festivals which are hardly celebrated today, but which can become beacons in the year for a child to look forward to.

Watching television

All parents must choose for themselves whether — and if so, how much — television is watched in the family. This will depend, among other things, on the place television has in the life of the parents and on the age of the children. A family with secondary school children will probably watch more TV than a family with toddlers. If you want to make a conscious decision about whether or not to watch TV in the family, you should ask yourself, above all, how child-friendly a TV is at this age, even if there are special programmes for toddlers and small children.

Only those things that can have a place in the real experiences of a child are really child-friendly. A toddler is open and accessible and imitates everything that he sees and experiences around him. He is not yet selective and does not have a critical faculty with regard to his impressions. This critical faculty develops by the time he goes to school. All impressions, including some that the toddler can't yet fully digest, are taken in. It is healthy if the impressions he experiences can be assimilated and digested. If they are not, it can have a negative effect, even at the physical level.

A small child has a 'magical consciousness,' a consciousness that is experienced in images. Father Christmas can travel over the rooftops and crawl down the chimney without any problems, while gnomes and dragons really exist. For the adult consciousness, with its realistic perspective and no nonsense attitude, these sorts of images are nonsense. We tell a child who is afraid of the dark, 'There are no dragons.' But this comment does not remove the child's fear, and clearly the experience of reality of a small child cannot be influenced so easily.

Conversely, the no nonsense world of the adult, in which technology, information and efficiency all have a place, is foreign to the toddler and difficult to integrate with his own experiences. If you want to create a child-friendly environment for your toddler, based on experiences of the world that he can comprehend at his young age, television, radio and computers don't fit naturally, even programmes that are specially made for children.

Magical consciousness is expressed in the imagination, which a child develops during the toddler years. When we tell a child a story, he produces his own imaginative images and is therefore being creative. Anyone who has ever seen the film version of a book he has read will be familiar with the shock of finding that the way in which he imagined it is completely different from the way in which it has been interpreted on screen. The opposite also applies: if you first see the film and then read the book, it's very difficult to allow your own imagination to work and to escape the insistent images of the film. On the basis of this experience you could say that all equipment that produces ready-made images and sounds to accompany a story prevents creative interaction with it. The imagination is one of the richest forces in childhood and is important for creativity in later life. We cannot escape the impression that TV, as well as radios and computers, are a fundamental threat to its development.

Another problematic aspect of TV is that it produces 'false' images. You do not hear the real voices of people on TV, or real musical instruments, but a physical representation. You do not see the newsreader, but a reproduction of him or her projected on to a flat screen consisting of pixels. We interpret these pixels as the newsreader and are barely aware that this is only part of reality. The situation becomes clearer when we watch nature films on TV. Whether these are pictures from the tropics or the poles, whether they show a storm or there is barely a breath of wind, we remain in our comfortable chair and do not experience what is being shown. It is natural for a child to use all his senses in the things he experiences. The child hears and feels the rain and the wind, smells the wet earth, feels cold and jumps up and down to get warm. The TV provides information that does not turn into a real experience of life for the small child, and with which he can do nothing. Too much of this sort of incomplete information can make the child feel uncertain.

As a third point, we would like to mention that an increasing amount of research demonstrates that watching TV has an effect on physical processes: a damaging effect on metabolism, circulation and the nervous system. For a toddler, life equates with movement; while he is moving, he exercises the senses and gets to know his body and therefore himself. We have already pointed out that it's essential for a child to have sufficient real experiences and to express these with his body. When he's watching TV, the child is motionless, the use of the muscles is reduced and the eyes are fixed on one point. It's clear that watching a lot of TV, in this unnatural, restrictive position, affects the way in which the child learns to use his body freely.

Because children can get 'glued to the box' and are therefore no problem at all for their parents, the TV is often used as a sort of babysitter. We believe that this in particular damages the child. The same applies for the use of computers at this age.

Finally, we would like to mention the negative influence that watching (a lot of) TV has on social life. Watching TV 'together' is an illusion. The TV demands everyone's attention and small children par-ticularly are absorbed by it. There is certainly no common activity, as there is when playing games to-gether. It's only when the TV is switched off that everyone focuses on each other again, and it is par-ticularly because of this last objec-tion that many parents choose not to have a TV at home.

If there is a TV, one good rule could be that the TV is switched on only when the youngest member of the family has gone to bed. In this way older children learn to consider the needs of their younger brother or sister, and the TV can also have a social function. You could also choose to have the TV in a bedroom rather than in the living room. This means that older children or par-ents can watch it without disturbing other family activities in the living room.

Safety

In every family there are situations in which a child just manages to avoid an accident, or when something bad happens but the consequences could have been much worse. In those cases, we could say that the child's guardian angel has come to his aid. For some people the child's guardian angel is a reality that gives confidence. For others, it's more an expression that's used in this sort of case. Whether it's a reality for you or not, you can talk about the accident afterwards with a sense of relief and gratitude. Obviously you cannot count on the child's guardian angel and it does not absolve you from the responsibility of taking safety measures when bringing up your children. The toddler stage, above all, is a stage in which it is necessary to take safety measures.

In general terms, you can ensure safety at three levels:

1. Purchase safety items such as a good bicycle seat, a safe stair-gate, or a rack around the cooker. These can prevent a number of accidents.

2. Teach children good safety habits and set the right example yourself. Make sure you know where your child is and what he's doing, although of course this isn't always easy.

3. Teach your child to obey you and later also to obey himself. You can lay the basis for this obedience during the toddler years. In addition, it is important for the child to become increasingly independent so that he learns to gain an insight into what he can do himself and into the dangers around him. Within certain limits, the child should be given the freedom to explore, no matter how frightening this can sometimes be. You literally and metaphorically have to learn to let go of your child, so that he can learn to jump, climb, cycle etc. Over-anxiety can have an inhibiting effect with regard to safety.

The child's nature has a big influence on safety. Some children only attempt something new when they are really able to. Often these are the children who start to walk a little bit later, but then manage to get it right in one go. Other children blindly throw themselves into the adventure and simply do not appear to see danger. They will climb up, but then can't get down again later, or they will go right up to a dog no matter how big it is. These children often only learn what danger is the hard way.

Most accidents happen as a result of falls, burns, choking, drowning and poisoning, usually in and around the house. The following chapters contain practical advice and list the most important points to be aware of and ways in which accidents could be prevented. On p. 148 a number of household remedies are listed, which can be used for minor injuries.

6. Practical Advice for One Year to Eighteen Months

Development

During this period the child learns to walk alone better and better and sometimes even learns to walk backwards. She can also crouch down. If there is a staircase in the home, he'll try to climb it. Estimating distances is still difficult. If the child wants to sit down, he'll land on a stool by more or less aiming backwards. She likes to pull or push things and move them about, but can also pick up crumbs from the floor with her thumb and index fin-

ger with minute concentration. The small child shows the first signs of 'self-sufficiency': she takes hold of a beaker herself to drink from it and makes attempts to eat with a fork or spoon. She likes to imitate the things her parents do in the home and join in with all the household tasks. Often she will prattle away at the same time in her own language. Very precocious children sometimes already use a few words, which may or may not be quite correct. In the first instance, talking develops purely on the basis of imitation, without the child directly assigning any meaning: she 'tastes' the words and enjoys them. During these six months the child starts to understand more and more words; her passive vocabulary is much larger than the words she uses herself.

Child and parent

For the first time the child becomes aware that she can cause things to happen herself. For example, if she throws a plate from the table to the ground, it makes a sound and the plate suddenly disappears. She starts to see the relationships between things, and this is endlessly explored. Nevertheless, at this age the child is still in the position where things simply happen to her and automatically evoke reactions of joy, anger, frustration or sorrow.

The child likes to carry out small tasks, such as 'Close the door, please' and 'Can you take this to the kitchen?' She can carry out this task with pride, beaming with pleasure.

This is the period when you talk a lot to your child and name things for him. That doesn't mean that a toddler needs everything to be explained to him. It's particularly important for the child that you pronounce things clearly without using childish words.

At this age, the presence of the parents or a very familiar person is still very important. Some children start to cry when their father or mother leaves the room or when they are in bed on their own at night. Gradually the realization develops that Dad and Mum are still there, even when you can't see them. A longer absence of both parents, for example, for a holiday, can seriously undermine this confidence and continue to have a negative effect for a long time.

Sleeping and waking

During this period there is often a transition to one nap during the daytime. Usually this transition takes place gradually. For a while it may seem as though the child is too small for one nap, but too big for two. She may manage for a few days with one afternoon nap, but then start to need two naps in order to catch up. Finally, when a child has only one nap a day, she often sleeps very deeply and finds it difficult to wake up afterwards.

He leads an intensive life during the day and this sometimes makes it difficult to leave the day behind her at bedtime. The bedtime ritual becomes important. Make sure this incorporates some set habits, but keep the ritual short and simple. It will always be possible to extend it, but shortening it is not usually accepted.

A child who moves about in bed and throws off the cover and gets cold will benefit from a woollen sleeping bag.

Some common problems related to going to sleep at this age include:

fears, dreams, waking up early and climbing out of bed.

When the child has fears or dreams it is often enough to spend a little while reassuring him. Taking her out of bed, giving him a drink or staying too long may wake him up completely and confirm that something really is wrong. A cuddle in bed, possibly a nightlight, and keeping the door slightly ajar can also help. For parents it's often a problem when a child wakes up early. Sometimes a really thick curtain to keep out the light may help, and in addition a firm attitude that it really isn't time to wake up yet.

For children who want to climb out of bed, the only thing that will help at this age is a crib with high sides so that they cannot get out. For determined climbers, low sides combined with a sleeping bag will not stop them.

Play and toys

On the one hand, a child's play consists of imitating everything she has seen happening around her, and on the other hand, it consists of random discoveries. By trying things out again and again, changes and variety develop in her play.

At this age a child needs household articles to play with, a box to put things in, a chest that can open and shut and something that she can fiddle with.

During this period the child wants to have the space to make her own discoveries. If she plays with official children's toys, she won't be interested in the instructions. Because she wants to examine everything, it's good if she can experience different sensations, such as playing with smooth and rough blocks, wet and dry sand, a light basket and a heavy chest, a soft toy and a hard ball.

In addition to moving about and discovering the 'big wide world', the playpen provides a safe, protected place, where the child can play in concentration with a few things.

At this age, it's still difficult for her to play on her own as older toddlers do. Joining in with everything that has to happen at home is the biggest incentive for playing.

When the child plays with her parents, favourites include physical games and tumbling, such as 'I'm gonna catch you ...'

Care

To prepare your child for brushing her teeth at a later stage, it's a good idea to start brushing your own teeth in her presence.

Bottles of juice, milk, sweetened tea or fruit juice can seriously damage the child's teeth (see p. 59). Only give your child a drink at set moments, for example, when you have a cup of coffee or tea yourself, and teach her to drink from an ordinary beaker. If the child finds it very difficult to let go of her bottle, it's sometimes easier to make sure that the bottle is simply lost, for example, by leaving it at a holiday home.

If the child has become used to a dummy, which we discourage, (see our other book, *Baby's First Year*), it's advisable to limit the use to just a few moments in the day, for example, when she goes to sleep. Remove the dummy from her mouth when she has fallen asleep. It's even better to get the child used to a cuddly toy or doll instead of the dummy.

It's not yet necessary to teach the child to stop sucking her thumb; at the latest, this should happen when the permanent teeth start to come through. If thumb-sucking is linked to a doll or a cuddly toy, it can be limited by leaving the cuddly toy in the bed during the daytime.

Both children who suck on a dummy and thumb-suckers can develop problems with the ear and respiratory passages in the longer term, as well as speech problems. If necessary, talk to your health advisor about what you can do about this.

Because children still play on the floor a lot during this period, and it's often cold and draughty and they put all sorts of things in their mouth, they regularly catch colds. Make sure the child is dressed warmly enough and that her lower body feels warm. At this age, the child can't usually blow her nose yet. Therefore make sure that you observe good hygiene and put some baby ointment or Vaseline on her cheeks so her face doesn't dry out too much.

The use of cotton wool buds to clean the ears is a terrible habit. This usually pushes the wax into the auditory passage, while it should naturally work its way out. Only wax in the earlobe should be removed with a piece of cotton wool or the corner of a flannel.

Make sure that socks are big enough; stretchy socks are not suitable because they pinch. Shoes are only necessary when the child is walking well (see p. 70). If the child has a walker, make sure that she also walks about enough on her own.

Safety

During this stage the child wants to put everything in her mouth and climb on everything. Parents have to be constantly vigilant to ensure he's safe. Make sure that she can't reach toxic substances, plants or ashtrays, and provide security on the windows, doors, staircases, balconies, cupboards etc.

Also make sure that all the electric plugs in the home are protected. Make the kitchen safe and ensure that the child cannot reach sharp knives or hot pans. In the living room, a tablecloth can be dangerous: a child can pull it over herself with the hot teapot and all the other things on the table. In the bedroom the child's crib should be safe and she should not be able to fall out or get stuck between the bars. Never allow the child to be in the bath on her own and make sure that she can't slip in the bath by sticking a non-slip mat to the bottom. Small objects lying around can be dangerous, particularly on the staircase.

A playpen can be a good place for the child at this stage. If the child is in the playpen for a little while every day, you don't have to constantly watch over her.

If there are pets in the child's environment (rabbits, hamsters, dogs, cats, canaries), it's advisable to find out if she could be allergic to them, which diseases can be transmitted by these animals and what precautionary measures you can take. Consult the vet about this.

Outdoors, ponds and ditches can be dangerous even if they are very shallow. Also make sure that you have safe child seats in the car and on the bicycle.

Food and eating habits

The child can now sit down at the table with her parents and enjoy the social aspect of eating together. It's usually still too early to really eat the same food.

Many families have their hot meal in the evening, while the child was probably used to having her hot meal at lunchtime during the first year. Changing to a hot meal in the evening together with the rest of the family has the advantage that the child enjoys the company, and this can stimulate her appetite. In addition it may involve less cooking work because she can already eat some of the vegetables and cereals that the family are eating (provided they are unsalted and well cooked). One disadvantage could be that in most families the hot meal is eaten quite late and the young child will then be too tired to eat. An advantage of having the hot meal at noon is that digestion is easier and the child eats more calmly, whereas she is usually more active in the evening. The right choice depends on the nature and sleeping patterns of your child and on your family circumstances.

One good compromise could be to give the child her own food early in the evening and then allow her to have a little nibble with the rest of the family later on.

During the toddler years, children generally start to eat slightly less, and in addition their appetite may sometimes vary. Respond to this by giving her slightly less in the first instance. It's better to have three small meals and two snacks between meals than an enormous plate of hot food. Furthermore, drinking a lot of juice can ruin her appetite.

Many children want to eat on their own at this age. In order not to lose control all together, using two spoons can be a solution: one for the child and one for the parent feeding her. Eating with the hands is another possibility, and you can indicate what is acceptable and what is not.

A clear ritual at the start and end of the meal helps the child to learn to stay at the table to the end of the meal. For a child of this age sitting still for fifteen to twenty minutes is quite an achievement.

Using a harness in the high chair from the beginning means that this will be accepted as the norm, and you won't have to endlessly remind the child to stay in her seat.

The diet could be as follows:

Breakfast: a bowl of porridge and/or bread with a beaker of drink. If the child only eats bread, a beaker of milk or yogurt finishes off the meal.

Coffee time: a rice cake, piece of toast or a breadstick with some herbal tea or juice.

Midday meal: hot meal or sandwiches and a dairy dessert.

Teatime: fruit snack and possibly something to drink.

Evening meal: porridge and some bread, possibly something to drink, or a hot meal with dairy dessert.

Porridge

After the first year, you can simply carry on with a bowl of porridge for breakfast, possibly combined with bread, unless the child prefers to eat only bread.

The porridge can be made of oat flakes, or instant cereal (see ur other book, *Baby's First Year*).

Bread

Most children are now sitting up straight in the high chair and no longer choke on bread. If the child is used to light brown bread and has learnt to digest this, you can start to feed her wholemeal bread. This can be yeast bread but can also be bread leavened with honey and salt or sourdough bread.

Toppings for bread

This could be butter with nut paste, quark mixtures, cheese, fruit, apple molasses or possibly honey.

Drinks

If the child eats only bread, it's a good idea to give her a beaker of milk afterwards. A child needs 400–500 ml ($^1/_3$–$^1/_2$ quart) of dairy products per day. Drinks for other times of day include herbal tea, fruit juice, or juice from fruit concentrate. Try to vary these and don't give more than one litre (one quart) of drinks per day in total.

It's better to drink after the meal so that the drink doesn't ruin the child's appetite and she chews well and doesn't rinse away the food.

Snacks

The following snacks are suitable: toast, rusks, crusts of bread, crispbreads, rice cakes and breadsticks. Make sure the food doesn't go down the wrong way, causing the child to choke. For a child who eats only small amounts at a meal, the snacks can be richer in calories. This should not take away the child's appetite for the next meal.

Hot meal

This can consist of vegetables and cereals enriched with some oil, or possibly butter or cream, and if necessary some cheese for taste.

Some cooked vegetables can now also be given so that the child becomes used to their individual flavours and coarser structure. When a new vegetable is introduced, a little bit of cream may help the child to get used to the taste, or the new vegetable can be mixed with a familiar vegetable.

When choosing vegetables, vary the three parts of the plant: the fruit, leaf and root. The presence of all three parts in the diet promotes balanced growth. Remember that various (particularly non-organic) vegetables contain nitrates. Give these vegetables less often and in smaller quantities (see p. 55).

Another possibility now is chewing on a raw carrot or slices of cucumber.

In addition to cereals you can now also give wholemeal macaroni or spaghetti and gradually introduce rice, millet or buckwheat cooked as a porridge. You can also see whether the child can digest bulgar wheat, couscous, and

quinoa (a cereal-like product) and likes them. It is still too early for other wholegrains.

Fruit snack

The fruit snack increasingly becomes a snack consisting of individual pieces of fruit rather than a whole meal consisting of fruit, cereals and dairy products. It should be just enough to satisfy the child until the evening meal, but without ruining her appetite.

Salt

At this age, salt can be used in moderation. In hot weather, a toddler needs some salt in her diet because she loses a lot of salt and moisture through perspiration.

Herbs

When the interest in food declines, herbs can make it more attractive. These should be 'warming' herbs, like dill, aniseed, and fennel. The child is still too young for spices such as pepper, nutmeg and cloves.

Sugar

It is still advisable to give the child as little white refined sugar as possible. However, you can use products such as barley malt syrup, corn syrup, maple syrup, concentrated fruit juice, raw sugar, citrus fruits or honey to meet the child's need for sweet food, provided they are not too sickly sweet. Fruit will also satisfy the child's cravings for sweet things.

The nightshade family

Of the nightshade family (potatoes, tomatoes, peppers, aubergines), we recommend only giving potatoes as a vegetable with the hot meal.

Pulses

In addition to cereals you can add some lentils to the hot meal. Other dried pulses are still too difficult to digest.

Eggs

You can use egg whites in meals, although there's no objection to leav-ing this out for a while. From the age of three, egg yolks can also be included in the diet

Fish

It's better not to eat fish too often because of the pollution in the water, but you can use farmed salmon and trout.

Meat

If you follow the lacto-vegetarian diet we propose, you will avoid meat entirely. If the child mainly eats potatoes rather than cereals, as well as bread, vegetables and dairy products, it's advisable to give her meat from time to time.

7. Practical Advice for Eighteen Months to Two Years

Development

The child now has a large number of motor skills, which will be increasingly perfected during this next stage. He can also carry out more and more simultaneous movements, such as looking round while he's walking, without falling.

The child now easily steps over a step in the doorway. Often he can walk up and downstairs holding on to the railing. When he starts to walk he needs a little while to get going, and once he's walking it's still difficult to stop. Going round a bend is also often difficult. He throws a ball with his whole arm and pushes the ball with his foot rather than kicking it.

Although he was already able to take off his shoes, he can now take off all sorts of other clothes. He can sit upright in the high chair without being held in place and is able to eat with a spoon, but not yet without making a mess.

During this period, the child discovers that everything has a name.

The number of words actively used and understood increases. He uses mainly practical words; abstract concepts are not yet a reality. He also gradually learns to point out parts of his own body when asked.

His understanding of language increases. This is expressed in short sentences such as 'Dad gone,' 'Go to Mum.' The difference in intonation clearly reveals whether these should be interpreted as a question, statement or command. The child can point to pictures in a book on request, leading to a primitive form of reading: the combination of a picture and a word. Looking at books, question and answer games, nursery rhymes and singing songs correspond with this stage of development, and nearly every child will enjoy those activities.

The so-called 'bedtime monologues' are wonderful for the parents to hear. In the evening, children often lie awake for quite a while, prattling away as they digest their day.

Child and parent

During this stage, the child believes that the world revolves around him. In principle there is no empathy with others or sharing with others. You cannot call on these qualities because the child doesn't yet have them. Other children, particularly babies, appear to be seen more as objects than as human beings. The child does notice that there can be a reaction when you prick or hit another person. He often elicits this reaction, but doesn't associate it with his own experiences of pain.

The child likes to do a great deal himself and experiment in all sorts of ways, but is very disappointed when he notices that he's not yet able to do something. Any help from others can meet with violent resistance. Fortunately it's usually easy to distract a child at this age.

The child still has a very limited memory and doesn't yet know what is allowed and what is not; he doesn't have his own brake to stop him doing things he shouldn't. By constantly removing him from places where he shouldn't be, and by showing him again and again what is allowed and what isn't, he will slowly learn.

He has difficulty with abrupt transitions and likes things to be finished. 'Finished' is a word that many children learn at an early stage and like to use enthusiastically. Finishing the meal with a ritual, for example, in the form of a song, a saying or a prayer can meet this need.

Although a child can usually do without his father and mother slightly more easily now, he still likes to have his parents around. At this stage of life, the child is around you all day long. This means that you'll have many moments to enjoy with your child, but it will be hard to find time for yourself. You will consciously have to create this time.

Sleeping and waking

At this age an afternoon nap is still necessary. Some children sleep so deeply in the afternoon that it's barely possible to wake them and they sleep away most of the afternoon. This makes it difficult to get to sleep in the evening. It often helps to put the child to bed earlier for the afternoon nap. If this doesn't work, you'll have to choose: either a shorter midday nap, or later to bed in the evening.

If the child finds it difficult to go to sleep in the evening, it's important to avoid any excitement just before bedtime. It can help your child to get to sleep if you're still close by doing something near the bedroom or tidying up just after putting him to bed.

Play and toys

Dragging things around, taking things apart, making a mess, joining in household chores and playing with sand and water are popular activities at this stage. In addition to ordinary household items (see p. 73) the child now also starts to appreciate real toys like dolls and dolls' accessories, toy animals, a ball, a shape sorter and toys to push and pull along.

He loves games like, 'I'm going to get you ...', tumbling, playing ball and hide and seek.

Care

Make sure that periods of activity and quiet alternate regularly, as well as periods of being alone and together, inside and outside. You can draw up a list for a few days to see how the day goes and whether these elements are in balance.

At this age the child needs a lot of room to play. Inside there should be places where he can do his own thing, and outside he should have the chance to walk, run, climb, etc. It's now possible to play at brushing teeth, but don't force anything. For the sake of safety, make sure the child never walks around with a toothbrush in his mouth (see p. 60).

Safety

On the whole, the elements mentioned for one year to eighteen months still apply for this age-group. The child still has little sense of danger. When he learns to open doors himself, the world becomes a bigger place. The garden has to be locked and the shed should also be made safe for the child. A pond in the garden should be protected with wire. In addition, make sure that the banister on the staircase is good and strong and that there are no beds or seats in front of windows that are left open or which the child can open himself.

Food and eating habits

Try to make sure that meals are quiet times so that the child is calm enough to bite and chew.

The quantities a child eats in a day are sometimes small. For some toddlers, two slices of bread, some fruit, 400 ml of dairy products, some cheese and a little bit of hot food with some oil is enough, while others eat much more. Differences between children can be considerable and only the real extremes should give cause for concern. At this age, children develop much stronger taste preferences and refuse to eat some foods that they enjoyed before. These foods can be left out of the diet for a while and then reintroduced after some time, possibly in a different form.

If a child is given a lot of snacks, this can take away a healthy appetite and he will only want to eat the food that he really likes. In that case, it's clear what to do. Limit the snacks to a little something at teatime or coffee time and make sure the child does not eat or drink anything for at least an hour before sitting down for a meal.

Apart from this, the diet doesn't change much, except that more vegetables can be given now (see the list of vegetables on p. 55).

You can make a cautious start on raw vegetables such as beetroot, carrots, endive, lamb's lettuce and ordinary lettuce cut very fine in small quantities.

For grumbly tummies it may help to include fennel seeds when cooking cabbage.

The diet could be as follows:

Breakfast: bread with a beaker of milk or a bowl of porridge.

Coffee time: tea or juice with a rice cake or similar.

Midday meal: bread with milk, or porridge.

Teatime: fruit and a beaker of something to drink.

Evening meal: hot meal of vegetables and cereals, possibly lentils supplemented with oil (perhaps butter or cream) and if necessary some cheese for flavour, and a dairy dessert. The hot meal can also be eaten at midday.

Here are two recipes which are examples of suitable meals for this age group, which adults will also enjoy.

Vegetable tart

Choose one or two vegetables and cook them until they're almost cooked.

For the base, mix 250 g (9 oz) of flour, possibly combined with oats, and 50 g (1 $^3/_4$ oz) of butter and add enough water to make a firm ball. Roll out this ball and cover the bottom and sides of a pie dish. Prick holes in the bottom with a fork.

Bake the crust blind for ten minutes in a pre-heated, moderately hot oven.

Then cover the base with the almost cooked, still warm vegetables. Pour a mixture of quark or cream and some cheese, combined with a tablespoon of flour, over this to cover the vegetables.

Bake the pie in the middle of a moderately hot oven for 10–15 minutes until it is cooked and is a light, golden brown in colour.

Apricot sauce

Soak four dried apricots cut into pieces in some water for one hour.

Measure 250 ml ($^1/_4$ quart) of water and add two tablespoons of flour, a dash of oil, 1–2 tablespoons of vegetable stock powder and the soaked apricots. Cook the sauce for ten minutes.

Flavour the sauce with concentrated apple juice and parsley.

Serve with some vegetables, cooked cereals and toasted, ground sunflower seeds to make a full, nutritious meal.

8. Practical Advice for Two to Three Years

Development

A two-year-old stands firmly on her feet; she can run (but not yet stop a ball or change direction), she can kick a ball without falling over and she is agile on the staircase. She can also open doors. Tottering on her toes, she grabs hold of the doorknob and the door opens, sometimes with the child walking backwards through it. During the course of this year the child learns to jump, stand on one leg and walk on tiptoe.

Her self-sufficiency increases. A two-year-old can take off most of her own clothes, while a three-year-old toddler can partly dress herself if the clothes are suitable. It's still quite difficult to pull on a pair of trousers because she has to stand on one leg to do this. Becoming potty-trained is another important step in becoming self-sufficient.

In her play we see increasingly high towers and more complicated structures. The child will start to look after her dolls, or run a garage business based on imitating others. A tricycle is usually moved along with the feet on the ground at first, but by the age of three some children are able to cycle with their feet on the pedals.

During the course of this year the child starts to form longer sentences, with the appearance of nouns, adjectives, verbs and a direct object. At the start of the year many children are already able to identify themselves with their own name. At some point during this year there is the great breakthrough when the child starts to use the word 'I.'

The child often creates new and completely original words. Words are often mispronounced. At this age children can become impatient if they can't immediately think of the word they want to say. Then they'll start to stammer. This is completely normal and usually disappears automatically. Take time to listen to your child properly and give her the necessary time to find the right words.

Memory continues to develop during this year. If the child is briefly distracted, she can quickly pick up the thread afterwards: she remembers what she was doing before. This is also clear from conversations with the child. For example, if you talk about the big dog you both saw on your walk, you'll see the recognition on her face: he'll know what you're talking about. Memory develops particularly with regard to routine in and around the home.

The child starts to really draw for the first time: horizontal and vertical lines, dots, scribbles and eventually circles.

Child and parent

During the second year of a child's life, every new word was a joy to hear. By now you sometimes feel overwhelmed by the never-ending flow of words from your toddler, and she demands that you listen. Because of all this talking, the child sometimes doesn't find time to eat or play. In that case you should point out that eating and talking do not go together, or that you're busy doing something yourself and that it's better not to talk for a while.

Correcting the child when words are mispronounced can make her feel insecure. She can't yet listen to herself critically and is mastering language purely by imitating. It's better to correct the incorrect word in the answer that you give: 'Mum, Linna dood.' 'Yes, Linda is good.'

Because the child is so able verbally, it can seem as though she understands a lot, and there's a danger that you expect too much of her as a result. For example, in the presence of one of the parents she knows what is allowed and what is not, but without that parent there, the brake is gone and she may do things that are forbidden. This is nothing to do with a bad upbringing or an underdeveloped conscience. At this age the child does not yet have a conscience of her own; the person bringing her up serves as her conscience.

At this stage she is quite self-sufficient, but again there's a fine line between asking too much or too little from her. It's a good idea to practise the skills that make the child more self-sufficient: these are part of everyday life and the child can be very proud of her new achievements. While she's playing, the toddler will often be prepared to learn something new, but when she has to, she soon becomes obstructive.

Making choices is another thing a toddler is not yet really able to do, for example, if she is asked to choose a garment from a range of clothes. Take the lead and choose for her. Try to introduce fixed habits on fixed days of the week, for example, chocolate spread on a slice of bread on Sundays and going to feed the animals on Wednesdays.

Abrupt transitions are difficult for a toddler. Suddenly wanting her to come and sit down for a meal while she's enjoying playing can lead to a temper tantrum. These situations can be prevented by preparing her for what's coming. There is already a dawning awareness of concepts such as 'now' and 'almost,' particularly when they are linked to a concrete example, such as, 'I'm going to lay the table now and then we'll eat.'

Sometime during the third year of life, the child starts to experience herself as 'I,' separate from the world around her. She says 'I' to herself and 'no' to the world. She wants to do everything herself and obstinately perseveres in this. In order to develop a healthy sense of self, the child needs limits and resistance. She will resist these limits, but at this age it is a healthy reaction to the healthy limits imposed by the people around her. If these are missing and no limits are imposed on the child, she will start to look for limits, for example, by behaving in an increasingly difficult and challenging way.

On the other hand, you should not be too strict on the child during this stage of development, and allow her sufficient freedom of movement. A fixed, clear timetable for the day will provide the toddler with the support she needs. Distraction, humour and creativity can prevent confrontations from leading to temper tantrums.

A real temper tantrum can be very dramatic. Suddenly the child behaves in a way that she never normally does, for example, by throwing things about or hitting her head against the floor. This can also be a traumatic experience for the child, and afterwards she will really need her parents to console her. If the temper tantrum is a reaction to something you've asked her to do and you become angry and start to shout, this will only make the situation worse. For most children a temper tantrum ends more quickly if you don't pay too much attention and simply allow the child to rage on until she stops. For other children it helps to hold them tight.

It's precisely because of the reaction it provokes that a temper tantrum can be a powerful way for a child to get what she wants. By responding as neutrally as possible to a temper tantrum and not deviating from the original rules, you do not give the child the opportunity to start using it as a powerful tool.

During this stage children still take everything very literally. For example, if you say, 'Suzie has fallen asleep,' the child may respond with, 'Ow!' Taking things literally in this way can also lead to anxieties. For example, when everything is flushed away in the toilet or the bathtub empties by swallowing up the water, she may fear that she, too, could be swept away. Listening carefully to what the child is trying to explain and then working out what she is afraid of can remove many of these fears. If you then discuss what can and what cannot be flushed away, this will help the child to overcome her toilet fears.

Sleeping and waking

At this age, children need a clear daily routine. If this is missing in the family for any reason, it will usually be expressed in restless nights.

Some children no longer want to sleep in the afternoon. This makes for a long day, and by the evening they may be so overtired that going to sleep becomes difficult or they wake up with a shock during the night. Try to keep the afternoon nap going by maintaining the time at which the child always goes to sleep, for example, immediately after the midday meal. It often helps if you set an example yourself by going to have a rest, perhaps together with your child.

Bad sleeping habits can develop at this age, which the child obstinately sticks to, and it can be exhausting for the parents. This is dealt with in more detail on p. 137.

It can be helpful to talk through the child's day before going to sleep: 'And then you went to see Grandad, and Grandad forgot the bread for the ducks,' and so on.

Fears can also keep a child awake. It's not always clear where those fears come from. If the child has watched television during the day, it can often be traced back to this, as experience has shown. The way in which the child cries usually shows whether she is crying because she's ill, because she's afraid or to get attention.

If the parent takes measures to improve sleeping at night, a fussy child may start to oppose this by shouting with rage. This is a healthy reaction. Although it may seem a very vehement reaction, rest assured that you are doing the right thing.

However, a child may also respond with panic, and you will be able to sense this from the way she's crying. If this happens, the best way to help is by showing a reassuring attitude: that everything is all right, and impress upon her that at night everyone should be asleep. If the fear can be identified, for example, if the child is afraid of a scary monster under the bed, you can put this fictitious monster out of the window as quickly as possible.

Play and toys

At this age, children like to play under the table or in a little hut. Now that the child is no longer using the playpen, she will express her need for limits and a cosy little place to play in this way. A play house or a covered clothes horse will meet this need.

It's best not to leave all the toys within the child's reach. Put some away so that you can vary the toys to meet the child's needs at different times.

It's an excellent idea to tidy up toys together with your child at the end of the day. As a child mainly plays with the things around her at this age, tidying up toys while she's playing can restrict her play.

A swing, a hobby horse, a tricycle and the toys mentioned for eighteen months to two years old (see p. 101) will meet the most elementary needs of the child. Every child differs in whether she likes to play with a doll and needs extra dolls' clothes or whether she prefers to play with (wooden) animals or with a train or cars.

At this age, children love to draw and paint and play with modelling wax and water (also see p. 77).

Toddlers like to play ball with adults and romp around, play tricks and do craftwork. In addition, many children love to read books, now that they can turn the pages over one by one and describe the pictures. Nursery rhymes and songs also remain popular.

Care

Most children learn to use a tricycle at this stage and this usually becomes their favourite way of moving about. In addition, try to make sure the child also walks, runs and climbs regularly. Ideally every child should spend at least an hour outside each day where she can move about to her heart's content.

At some point during this year, take your child to the dentist when you go for a check-up yourself. She can then get used to it quietly before she has to go herself for the first time at the age of three.

If children are overactive or listless, make sure they are not too cold or dressed too warmly. Long hair in front of the face can be irritating or make children lethargic. Cutting or plaiting the hair or tying it up in a ponytail can sometimes have a miraculous effect.

Toilet-training is an important step forward in becoming independent. Most children become toilet-trained in the daytime during their third year of life, and become toilet-trained at night during the following years (see also p. 65).

Safety

In addition to the safety measures already mentioned for children aged one year to eighteen months (see p. 94), there are now a few other points for attention. As she is now good at climbing, the child can reach many things that are high up. Given the chance, she'll open doors and drawers to examine everything she can find.

At this age it's still not possible to leave the child on her own in the bath or in a paddling pool. Ponds in the area are still dangerous for her.

On her tricycle, the toddler really feels as if she's part of the traffic, but you still can't make agreements with her about what she is and isn't allowed to do. During the toddler stage, playing in the street is only safe if there really is constant super-vision.

Food and eating habits

The child can now eat meals using a fork or spoon, making much less of a mess. Drinking from a beaker has also become much easier.

At this age most children eat the food served for the main meal. In principle, the composition of the food remains unchanged. The way in which you serve it depends to a great extent on what works during this difficult period when the child will often say 'no' to food. This can lead to problems, particularly with hot meals. Suddenly the child refuses things that she was eating quite happily before. This requires a lot of creativity and flexibility on your part. You can't force the child to eat, but you can create the right conditions.

A number of tips:

• Keep up the eating habits that have been built up over time. If a child has become used to staying at the table until the meal has finished, refusing to eat should certainly not be rewarded by being allowed to leave the table earlier.

• Serve small portions, for example, one tablespoon of hot food and one tablespoon (or slightly more) of dessert.

• Keep an eye on snacks and don't give the child anything to eat or drink less than an hour before meals.

• Watch the amount of milk a child drinks; some poor eaters can drink as much as one litre (one quart) a day. Reduce it to no more than a half a litre a day so that the child can develop a healthy appetite again.

• Making the meal look attractive can help the child to accept it. It may also help to hide less popular vegetables and so on, for example, in puréed soups or cereal/ vegetable cookies (see recipe below).

• Playing outside before the meal can contribute to a healthy appetite. However, some children have to recover from playing outside before they can eat, so they should come inside half an hour before the meal.

• If you're eating a hot meal in the evening, try to do this early. Many children are simply too tired to eat after six o'clock, particularly if they haven't had a very long nap in the afternoon.

• If a child has not finished her food, it usually works best to clear the plate from the table without making a big deal about it.

Many children start to eat again after a period of refusing food, particularly when life is calm and there's a good atmosphere at the table. If eating continues to be a cause of concern, you can discuss your concerns at the child health centre (also see p. 136).

If your child goes to a crèche or toddler group, you could try giving her something to eat there that she refuses at home. In general the child will be more inclined to eat it in a strange situation.

A way of attractively dressing up vegetables:

Cereal/vegetable cookies

2 tablespoons of flour and/or oats soaked in some hot water or vegetable stock for one hour

1 tablespoon of ground hazelnuts or almonds

cooked puréed vegetables suitable for this age

a dash of oil, 1 tablespoon of grated cheese, 1 tablespoon of quark and some parsley or coriander

Mix up all the ingredients. Shape the dough into cookies the size of biscuits and fry them in a little oil until golden.

Sweets and treats also start to play a role, as children become more interested in them and they are offered more often. There's an art to providing a 'healthy' treat. When children have sweets it's best to enjoy them with conviction and without a bad conscience, as an exception to ordinary life. For the teeth it's better to eat sweets once to your heart's content and brush your teeth afterwards, than to eat small amounts throughout the day.

9. Practical Advice for Three to Four Years

Development

The movements become more supple and secure. The child can now walk up the stairs with one foot on each step, although he can't yet do this going downstairs. He can kick a ball in the desired direction and he can also catch a large ball with his arms outstretched. The degree of self-sufficiency increases further. He is now able to undo buttons and laces, and most children also become potty-trained at night during this year.

The memory also continues to develop. Adults can remember things from their childhood from this age. In addition, the child can now remember abstract things for the first time, such as numbers.

The child constructs more complete sentences, including words like 'yesterday' 'tomorrow' 'because' 'but' 'if' 'or' 'who' 'what' 'where' 'why' 'when' and 'how.' The use of these sorts of words shows the child's increasing understanding of the world. Using the words 'if ... then' shows that he can place things within time — admittedly at a childish level — and that he has a dawning awareness of cause and effect. He also learns to use the terms 'we' 'you' 'mine' and 'yours' correctly. The child now realizes that the whole world does not belong to him, but that things belong to other people and that you are therefore not allowed to touch everything. The child now mispronounces fewer words, but because he wants to speak at the same rate that the words come into his head, he may often stammer. By no means all the grammatical rules are applied correctly yet.

This is also the age when children enjoy saying 'pee' and 'poo' and love to use other rude words.

By the age of four, the child starts to think independently for the first time. This is the age of the never-ending 'Why?' Sometimes it's as though he's not really interested in the answer (a typically adult point of view), but with enjoying the new possibility of asking the reason for things.

In his drawings he produces the first people, with just heads and legs.

When the child reaches the age of four he is leaving a stage behind him and preparing for a new life, the life of the small child. The child uses the word 'I', speaks clearly with main sentences and relative clauses and uses adjectives. In his games, his own creativity flourishes and he does not constantly have to be shown how to do things. Picture books have a clear significance and can be 'read.' The related story is recognized and variations on the story are loudly commented on and usually rejected.

Child and parent

When the child uses the word 'I' all the time and the sense of self becomes increasingly strong, the period of saying 'no' is gradually left behind. This is the start of a stage in which the child becomes more cooperative. A three-year-old is more self-controlled and is better at waiting, because he has started to understand what is meant by 'now' and 'later.' Gradually he learns to follow the rules, even when his parents are not around.

For the first time, the child can also start to feel guilty about things. You could say this is the emergence of a conscience, but it's still an early stage and you should not appeal to it yet. Firstly, he cannot adapt rules on the basis of his own insight: if a child has learnt the rule that he must never take anything away from someone else, he may stick to the rule when a little brother or sister has got hold of a knife. He's not able to judge what's actually most important at that moment. In addition, this is the age at which children are so keen to do their best that they can be over-demanding of themselves. In this case, appealing to the child's feelings of guilt is a very heavy burden. You can meet the needs of the child better by praising him and giving him compliments that you really mean.

By the age of four, the child also starts to take other people into account. This is the end of a period in which he mainly approached the world from an egocentric point of view. In addition, he is now aware that other people have feelings.

A three-year-old is usually able to achieve quite a lot verbally. If something is not allowed and the child does not agree, this can lead to long discussions. If you go along with this as an adult, you will never have the last word. You can become entangled in arguments with endless 'Why?' questions. Discussions are fine and also necessary at this stage, but sometimes it's not the right moment for them and the child simply has to be quiet and listen. This can be the first sign of real obedience, which is very important, for example, for safety in the street.

A child can get so good at conversation that it's easy for parents to forget that a child of almost four still lives in a very different world from an adult. The child lives in his imagination, and the laws of logic that apply for us do not apply for him. By looking carefully at what the child shows in his games, and by listening to what he's asking, you can get much closer to him. Often the things that bother him or the fears he has can be better understood. The questions that a child may ask at this stage about birth and death and about the meaning of things are often very big questions. The child needs the help of an adult who will listen carefully and try to find out where the question is coming from, without necessarily filling in all the pieces straightaway. You can discuss these subjects with your child without having ready-made answers; tell him that you also find these questions difficult and want to think about them for a while.

Sleeping and waking

In many cases, the afternoon nap comes to an end during this year, because the child no longer wants the nap or because an afternoon nap leads to problems with going to sleep in the evening. Try to maintain the good habit of getting the child to do something by himself in a quiet place at the time of the afternoon nap, for example, in his own room. This can become a beneficial point of rest during the day, both for the child and for you.

A good bedtime ritual in the evening, which stops the child making all sorts of demands, continues to be important.

In bed the child may start to need a pillow because of the changing position of the head in relation to the shoulder. A thin pillow is most suitable, while a feather one is too hot.

If the child is now potty-trained during the night, it's important that he can easily take off his pyjama trousers and get out of bed by himself. In this respect, a bunk bed will lead to problems.

At this stage, the child may also still wake up with fears in the night (see p. 108).

Play and toys

During this year, the child's games enter a new, rich stage as imaginative play develops. Everything is involved in the game; chairs and tables and pieces of material are needed to make an imaginary house with planks and blocks to make the roads to the house, while the carpet is the sea, and watch out, because if you walk on it you'll get wet feet! In this way the child builds his own world and you can almost feel like a stranger in that world. By joining in the game, and only walking over the water on the bridge when you have to go by, you won't disturb him.

In addition to the toys mentioned before, the child now needs things that fit into this new game. Dressing-up clothes and pieces of fabric are important accessories, as well as dolls, cooking things, accessories for a conductor on a train or a doctor's case. By the age of four when the child is ready for nursery school, he can sometimes be ready to play and share toys with other children. This ability will develop, particularly with a good example and a loving environment.

At this age children enjoy craft activities, but they still need some-one to help them with this.

At the end of this year some children are ready for real group games. They are able to keep to simple rules and enjoy playing together.

Care

The child can now wash himself a little under supervision and can mainly dress himself. But, as before, what the child can do himself still doesn't have to become a rigid duty. Some children are slow to get going in the morning and sometimes you simply won't have time to allow him to do everything by himself, and you'll have to help. Other children are so tired by the evening meal that they can't finish their meal themselves and still need help with feeding.

Many children have cold, clammy feet. Wash their feet regularly and make sure they have clean, warm socks every day.

Activities may be available in your local area in which movement has a central place, such as gymnastic classes for toddlers. This is often a wonderful activity for children who have bags of energy.

Almost all children will be potty-trained during the day by now. Over the course of the fourth year most children are also dry at night. If a child has only just been potty-trained during the day, don't wait too long to see whether he can manage at night as well — a few wet sheets will usually be enough to get this going. For a little while you can leave the nappy on at night and put the child on the toilet or potty as soon as he wakes up. Consider taking the child out of bed in the evening to take him to the toilet. The right moment for this will be different for every child. For some children this may be just one hour after going to sleep. It's important to wake the child briefly before going to the toilet or he will learn to urinate in his sleep. Some children learn to be dry at night more quickly if they are woken up.

If a child suggests that he wants to sleep without a nappy it's certainly worth considering, even if it does lead to a few wet sheets. You can buy under-sheets impregnated with rubber to protect the mattress. Sometimes you'll still have to take the child out of bed in the evening for quite a while as he gradually adapts.

There's no point in not allowing the child any drinks in the afternoon in order to keep the bed dry; this can quickly lead to the issue becoming a sensitive.

At the age of four there are still many children who are not dry at night; bedwetting is only officially used to describe a problem from the age of six or seven onwards. Most children manage to become dry at night by themselves before that age.

Safety

As regards safety, three-year-olds can't be trusted. Therefore the safety measures mentioned for the previous stages continue to apply.

Food and eating habits

Although many children now eat everything their parents eat, and the habit of saying no has usually disappeared, it's not realistic to expect a child to like everything or to always finish his meal. Even for an adult this is sometimes too much to ask.

A lacto-vegetarian diet is still desirable, but in principle a child can now eat everything. Each child's diet should be assessed on an individual basis, and the child himself will indicate what he does and does not want to eat. With regard to the child's preferences, it's a good idea to ensure these are not one-sided and to discourage one-sided development.

The basic diet continues to consist of three main meals and two snacks, or four meals.

Bread

The child can now chew so well that he can also eat coarse wholemeal bread and possibly also nut bread or bread with seeds.

Dairy products

300–500 ml ($^1/_3$ quart–$^1/_2$ quart) of dairy products per day is still desirable. If the child eats a lot of cheese (for example, three slices of bread with cheese) or quark (a bowl), they can drink less milk.

Cereals

Oats and barley can now also be cooked with whole grains but thermo-cereals are still preferable because they are easier to digest. In addition, pasta (macaroni, spaghetti) and cereals cooked with vegetables are suitable.

Pulses

These are not essential. Dried pulses are fairly difficult to digest, though in principle a child should be able to digest them well at this stage.

Herbs

Gradually more herbs can be added to food, but be restrained when using hot spices and herbs. The child's taste will become less acute if these are used.

Salt

Use salt in moderation, though slightly more for dreamy children. Remember that the kidneys cannot yet process large amounts of salt.

Eggs

One egg a week is sufficient, for example, as a special treat for breakfast on a Sunday morning. Use eggs in other meals in moderation.

Fish

At this age children do not yet have to eat fish, but it can be a solution for fussy eaters.

Meat

A lacto-vegetarian diet is sufficient and meat is not necessary, but if the child does eat meat, it's advisable to use organic or biodynamic meat.

Vegetables

All varieties of cabbages, leeks and onions can now be eaten, possibly in soups. By using herbs such as fennel, cumin and aniseed, many things that are difficult to digest can be made more digestible. Raw vegetables can now become a fixed part of the diet, as well as cooked vegetables.

10. Looking After Sick Children

Pain and fever

The most common symptoms of illness in small children are fever and pain.

Fever is a mechanism of the body's immune system, used to combat a perceived threat inside the body, such as bacteria or a virus, as effectively as possible. It is not a disease in itself but the body's response to a disease. In itself, a high temperature is not dangerous. Unfortunately there is a widespread fear of fever. Firstly, this is because fevers can cause convulsions, but in reality these occur rarely and only when a fever is rising. Once a child is ill, the danger of convulsions has passed, no matter how high the temperature. It is often incorrectly thought that a child who has had convulsions is also at a greater risk of becoming epileptic. In principle, convulsions are not harmful, although they are always a frightening experience for parents.

When your child is ill, give her small amounts to drink more often. With a fever, sweet drinks, for example, herbal tea with some honey, are preferable because the sweetness increases blood-sugar levels and this helps a child to cope with a rapidly rising temperature. Don't force her to eat. In addition, some parents believe that problems with the brain, the heart or other vital organs can occur as a result of a fever. This is completely incorrect. It's only the illness that causes the fever that can be dangerous, for example, meningitis. But in that case a child will show other symptoms as well. Many children have periods of fever for which there is no explanation. When they have a high temperature look at the other symptoms — congestion, coughing, urinary complaints or drowsiness — to assess how ill the child is. Consult someone in good time to overcome your concerns, but don't be afraid of fever in itself.

Suppressing a fever has many disadvantages but few advantages. The temperature goes down and then rises again, and it's precisely because of this that you feel unwell. We have already pointed out the importance of fever for the immune system; by suppressing fever the immune system becomes less efficient. Lemon socks (see p. 145) are recommended for a feverish or restless child. This doesn't always bring down the temperature, but it often makes the child feel better, which in turn can bring the fever down.

Many illnesses are accompanied by pain. It can be useful to take measures against pain so the child feels more comfortable, but also to make sure everyone gets a good night's sleep.

A number of simple remedies are as follows:

• Heat can help ease a stomach ache, toothache or a sore throat (heated bandages, see p. 146).

• Cold, usually in the form of cold water or an ice compress (see p. 146), can work well in the case of sprains, bruises or pulled muscles. Don't simply put the ice on the injured place. It's best to dab the injury gently, but for no more than fifteen minutes. This can then be repeated later.

• Arnica works surprisingly well on bruises and injuries where the skin is not broken.

• For earache, applying an onion compress behind the ear (see p. 145) is a tried and tested remedy for pain and ear infections.

If none of these things help, you can give some pain relief by way of medicines. You should be aware when you do this, probably in order to give you and your child a well-needed rest, that the pain relief medicine is not curing the illness.

The family doctor

Parents know their child best and are often the first to feel that something is wrong. Intuitively you may also know whether it's serious or not. Parents are emotionally involved with their children and therefore they are not the appropriate people to make a diagnosis, also because they do not have the required medical knowledge. This is what doctors are for. You can save yourself a great deal of uncertainty by consulting the family doctor in good time. This will make you feel calmer and more confident, and that's very important for a sick child.

Complaints and illnesses

The baby years are characterized by growth, and the child learns to know and use her own body. Normally there are very few illnesses during this time, but that tends to change during the toddler years. The child starts to discover the world around him, and the various contagious illnesses with which she comes into contact are part of this. It's fairly normal for a child to regularly have a runny nose or be ill. By supporting her resistance with good clothes and food, making sure she regularly goes outside and providing an appropriate lifestyle, you give her the chance to learn to overcome illnesses. When his resistance is lowered, for example, by vaccinations or events that have a big impact, medical support may be helpful.

This chapter deals briefly with a number of illnesses and complaints that are common in the toddler years, and advises what you can do about them. We are aware that because this chapter is brief, the reader may well be left with questions. Our aim is to provide a general overview of what you can do for a sick child using anthroposophical and natural medicines, and with external treatments (see p. 143). For more detailed information, see the bibliography.

Coughing

Many small children cough a lot, whether or not they have a cold. This is quite normal at this age and therefore only requires medical treatment in special circumstances. An important consideration is whether there's a history of asthma, hay fever, allergies or infantile eczema in the family. If there is, the coughing may be a sign of the same predisposition in the toddler and treatment may be required. If it's accompanied by a fever that does not subside within three days, always consult a doctor. Don't mess around with cough mixtures yourself. For whooping cough, see p. 129.

The common cold

This is very common in small children and quite harmless. However, if a child constantly has a cold, you should consult a doctor.

Symptoms of a cold are an unpleasant green discharge from the nose, smelly breath, and the adenoids are usually infected, even with a normal temperature. Nose drops made of camomile tea or physiological salt are useful first-aid remedies that you can make yourself. Drip three drops in each nostril six times a day. Applying a little bit of cream into each nostril before going to bed makes it easier for the child to breathe when he's asleep.

Middle-ear infection

This is probably the most common illness in small children. Often it happens after the child has had a cold, and the enlarged adenoids or an adenoidal infection can play a role. The child suddenly has earache and a fever and is quite deaf. The pressure on the ear passage hurts and the child is ill and often cries.

The course of the illness can vary. After a few hours it may disappear of its own accord and never come back, but it can also be the start of a problem that can continue for years, and in a few cases, it may be necessary to insert grommets in the eardrum.

In the first instance, it's sufficient to treat the pain (onion behind the ear) and give nose drops (physiological salt). If this doesn't help, consult a doctor. Sweet milk products can promote the production of mucus and therefore it's better to use sour milk products in the diet.

Deafness

This is very common during and after an acute middle-ear infection because it causes moisture behind the eardrum (glue ears). This deafness disappears spontaneously within three months in almost all children. If it lasts much longer (for example, as the result of yet another ear infection) and the child's speech development is affected, she no longer functions well socially or her general health is suffering, inserting grommets may be a solution.

Swollen glands

These are very common in toddlers. This applies to the glands in the neck, particularly at the corner of the lower jaw. Usually this is quite harmless and gets better by itself, but there are two important exceptions:

• Infection of the lymph nodes in the neck — this usually occurs on one side, but sometimes on both sides. This infection leads to extremely large glandular swellings. In a one-sided infection, the child's head is constantly at an angle. The symptoms are usually a fever and pain. Consult the doctor.

• Acute sore throat — a painful infection of the adenoids. A child will have about 38.5° C (100° F) fever, a sore throat and it hurts to swallow. Often she doesn't want to swallow and can't swallow her own mucus either, and she will start to dribble. Again, consult the doctor.

Croup

This is a viral infection of the larynx (Adam's apple). It's usually very acute, particularly on warm, humid evenings. The child's breathing feels constricted, she can become anxious and restless and has a strange rough, barking cough. She may also have a fever. The symptoms may be so extreme that the parents panic, but this only makes things worse. One tried and tested treatment is a steam bath. Take the child to the bathroom, put on the warm shower and hold her on your lap. Singing a song or rocking her will make her feel at ease. Usually she'll quickly feel better. Of course, you'll not feel so comfortable yourself; it may feel like a sauna. When the congestion has reduced, the child can go back to bed. Usually she'll continue to be hoarse for a while and she may have more coughing fits and fever. Generally these symptoms disappear over the following days without leaving any trace. As this illness looks so severe, it's a good idea to consult the family doctor. She can often diagnose croup coughing over the telephone and give advice.

Impetigo

This infection usually occurs around the mouth or nostrils. Red patches, yellow crusts and the appearance of pussy blisters are the most characteristic signs. It's very contagious! It is caused by bacteria invading the skin through a cut or skin infection. It can be passed on by children who have a nail or throat infection, as the same bacteria are involved. Consult the doctor.

Lice

Head lice are very common in primary school children, but even at a younger age a child may find that these 'guests' pay a visit. You can catch lice by wearing someone else's hat or from a cuddly toy or cushion. Lice are small grey creatures, which are visible to the eye. They are about the size of a match-head. The louse lives on the blood that it sucks from the skin on the head. These wounds can itch, but many children have no symptoms. The female lays her eggs (nits) in the hair. The nits are white or light yellow, approximately 1 mm long and hatch after seven to ten days.

When tackling head lice, you should take into account the child herself and the people around her who may be contaminated. Anyone who has been in contact with the child should be checked. Washing at 60° C (140° F) is sufficient for clothes that could host lice. Clothes or bedding can also be put away in a sealed plastic bag for a week. The fastest treatment for a child is to shave off all the hair, but this is rather extreme. Instead you can patiently comb the hair with a louse comb (in particular, the Nisska make) every day for a fortnight. Dipping the comb into a bowl of vinegar solution will help. This treatment always works, but takes a lot of time and patience.

Anti-lice remedies easily penetrate the skin and are therefore not recommended.

Worms

Many toddlers suffer from worms. Usually these are threadworms: 1 cm ($1/_3$ inch) long, white, threadlike worms, which can be seen in or on the faeces. The child may have an itch around the anus and a tummy ache and girls can contract a vaginal infection. Many natural remedies have been developed to help get rid of them, but our experience shows that only 'anti-worm' medicines are really effective. Your pharmacist will be able to advise. The view that worms are related to poor hygiene is not confirmed in practice. However, worms are contagious and often several members of the family will be contaminated.

Bladder infection

This is mainly a girls' complaint. The main symptoms are that urinating is painful and girls have to go more often or feel the need, but can't go. If there's also a fever, that completes the symptoms. If possible, remove all sugar from the diet and give the child a lot to drink. Acidic vitamin C-rich drinks such as orange juice and cranberry juice make the urine acidic, and help the infection to get better on its own. However, the urine should be checked by the doctor. In addition, it's important to keep the lower body and legs warm, for example, with woollen tights and warm socks.

Vomiting

A child over the age of one doesn't become dehydrated very easily. Many children are sick from time to time. Watch out for the following symptoms. In general, vomiting without a fever and diarrhoea is harmless. Vomiting with a fever usually indicates an (intestinal) infection. When the vomiting is accompanied by a fever and diarrhoea keep a careful eye on things and consult the doctor.

One of the dangers of considerable vomiting is dehydration. Fever can be a symptom of dehydration, but a child who urinates less than twice a day, cries without tears or is generally dopey are also alarm signals. In that case you should certainly consult the doctor.

If no symptoms ring alarm bells, a short period of fasting will probably be enough. Don't allow the child to eat or drink for three to six hours, but she could rinse out her mouth, for example, with apple juice. When the vomiting has stopped, start with half a beaker of fennel tea or camomile tea. Another good recipe is rice water (the leftover water from boiling rice) mixed with equal parts of stock. A camomile wrap or compress on the tummy can sometimes work miracles. If the child feels better she can have something easily digestible and savoury to eat. If there's no improvement after half a day, consult the doctor.

Diarrhoea

The term 'diarrhoea' refers to watery stools, which occur more than four to six times a day. When this occurs in combination with vomiting and a fever, the doctor should be consulted. If this is not the case, you can treat it with a short period of fasting, as with vomiting. Norit or birch charcoal (Carbo Betulae powder) can be efficient remedies, as can a camomile wrap or compress. If the child responds positively to this, you can feed her thin gruel made of diluted milk, yoghurt, stock, herbal tea or possibly weak black tea. The next day the diet can be extended with light, low-sugar products such as (toasted) white bread, soft vegetables and white rice. Cooked carrots and uncooked grated apple are good for unsettled intestines. If the diarrhoea stops, you can move back on to light brown bread, but for a few days you should avoid stimulating

or heavy food. On the other hand, if the diarrhoea persists, consult the doctor.

If the stools are viscous, this is not diarrhoea. Many small children produce viscous stools. If the stool smells sour or rotten or consists of poorly digested food, it's useful to look at the child's diet together with the doctor or nurse at the child health centre. An unbalanced diet that contains too little fat or too much sugar, or a diet too rich in fibre or large quantities of apple juice, can thin the stools (although this is less common if the apple juice is organic apple juice).

Constipation

During the first four years, the child's stools naturally become thicker. Constipation occurs when stools get very concentrated and hard, causing bowel movements to become painful and occur less often, or stop altogether. If there are no bowel movements for a few days, the tummy can feel quite hard. The child does not feel well and loses her appetite. A hot-water bottle and a camomile wrap on the tummy, and warm feet and legs can stop the cramp.

The causes of constipation can be: a constipating diet, not enough to drink, painful bowel movements, not enough exercise, too much excitement and tension. If a child is constipated for a long time, the intestines become overfull and she can only pass some thin faeces, signs of which are then found in her underwear.

A diet high in the following foods may cause constipation: all foods containing white sugar and flour, bananas, toast, cinnamon, grated apple, chocolate, rice cakes. In this case, wholemeal products and fresh fruit and vegetables can help to remedy the constipation. Citrus fruits, beetroot, soaked dried prunes, oats and sour-milk products stimulate the intestines.

Not drinking enough can also lead to constipation. A child who tends to become constipated needs to drink at least one litre (one quart) of fluids per day.

In some cases there are small cracks in the anus and the child will hold back the impulse to push for as long as possible. In that case you should consult the doctor.

In addition, exciting events such as moving house or starting a new toddler group, tension in the family or strict potty-training can cause constipation. Try to remove the tension and make sure you provide sufficient fluids and a laxative diet.

First-aid

A few words of advice are given below, which may be useful in the case of common accidents in the home, garden or kitchen. These recommendations can never replace expert medical advice.

Nosebleeds

Children quite often have nosebleeds. Ask the child to blow her nose until it's completely empty, then pinch the nose tightly for five minutes just below the hard bony part. Keep the child's head bent slightly forward while she's sitting up straight. This procedure sometimes has to be repeated a number of times. There is no need to be afraid of a nosebleed as long as the nosebleed lasts no longer than one hour. If it lasts longer, consult a doctor.

Concussion

The symptoms of concussion are: a loss of consciousness immediately after the blow (out for a moment) and/or vomiting within a few hours. A headache is not necessarily a symptom. A fever can develop within twenty-four hours, sometimes as high as 40° C (104° F).

Make the child rest. Avoid any sensory stimulation caused by noise, television etc. Apply an Arnica compress to the forehead (with diluted Arnica essence 20%), or if this is not available apply 10% Arnica ointment. Also give ten drops of Arnica D3 six times a day. If it was a very hard blow, it's advisable to wake the child every two hours the following night. This prevents internal bleeding in the skull, which may occur later if the concussion goes unnoticed. In that case, the child can no longer be woken up and medical help must be sought immediately.

Insect bites

Ticks can transmit Lyme disease, a disease that can eventually lead to inflammation of the joints and neurological complaints. For this reason, ticks should be removed as quickly as possible. Remove the tick with tweasers or pliers and then disinfect the area where it was found. Use of alcohol or oil will cause the tick to empty its stomach, which actually promotes Lyme disease. A tick must have been on the skin for more than twenty-four hours to transmit the disease. After removing the tick and disinfecting, no further treatment is necessary. If a red swelling gradually develops around the tick bite in the following weeks, consult a doctor.

In the case of wasp or bee stings, remove the bee's sting, but do it correctly. If the poison sac is still connected to the sting and you pinch it with tweasers, you're helping to give the victim an extra dose of poison. Therefore take hold of the bee sting itself with your pincers. Then suck out the place where the child was stung with a powerful suck. If this leaves a mark, you'll know that you've sucked hard enough. Then you can treat the place with Combudoron ointment for burns or with Combudoron spray.

Other insect bites can be treated with the same remedies. Witch hazel cream helps to combat the itching.

If a child responds to an insect bite with violent physical reactions, contact the doctor.

Itching

Itching is very common. There can be countless reasons for this, which are often unimportant. Menthol powder or applying Combudoron liquid for burns diluted in the ratio 1:10 helps very quickly.

Burns

Immediately rinse burns on the open skin with cold water for fifteen minutes. If the burn is covered by clothes, be careful. Synthetic fibres can melt and burn into the skin. In that case, don't remove them. You could unnecessarily deepen the burn by pulling the skin off with the clothes. Rinse the skin and the clothes together. If the clothes are made of natural fibres you can remove them without any risk, so that the burn can be treated.

Superficial burns (first degree), which affect only the surface of the skin, making it red, swollen, and painful, can be treated at home, provided that you ensure the wound is clean. First apply cold, wet Combudoron compresses (with diluted Combudoron liquid for burns). This has to be refreshed as soon as the burn starts to hurt. Combudoron gel for burns also has a cooling effect. Afterwards treat the place with Combudoron ointment for burns.

Deep or large burns, or burns to the face, hands or across joints must always be checked by a doctor and may require hospital treatment.

Remember that a lot of pain doesn't necessarily mean that it's a serious burn; it's precisely the superficial burns (first degree) that hurt a lot because the nerves are still intact. In deeper burns these have been damaged and the wound becomes less painful.

Poisoning

Always consult the doctor. You can buy a guide to poisons, which will give you some useful tips.

Sprains and pulled muscles

Arnica is the best remedy for these sorts of injuries. To counter the worst pain and swelling apply a cold, wet Arnica compress with diluted Arnica essence (20%). Then apply Arnica ointment (10%) thickly to the painful place and bandage it up.

Cuts

Rinse cuts with tepid water, pat them dry and put on a plaster. The bleeding will usually stop after five minutes.

Infected wounds or patches

One night with a bandage soaked in camomile tea or Calendula (Calendula essence, 20% diluted) is often sufficient to treat infected wounds or patches. Do not encase the wet bandage in plastic. When the infection has disappeared the wound can be treated with Calendula ointment.

Sunburn

Children are usually more sensitive to the sun than adults. In recent years there has been a great deal of publicity warning that too much sun is bad for our health. You have to be extra careful with children. You can tell whether a child has had too much sunlight not only from their skin but also from reactions such as headaches and nausea. In that case, it's important to immediately remove the child from the sun. Fortunately, many children seek out shade themselves. On the beach, always make sure the child is wearing a sunhat, provide some shade and give the child enough clothes to cover up in good time. Use a sun cream of SPF 30 or higher. Red skin can be treated in the same way as superficial burns (see p. 127).

The childhood diseases

When a child contracts a childhood disease it usually has a big impact. In the first place, there's the fact of being ill itself. Most children often have clear memories of their measles, mumps, chicken pox, etc. Secondly, this can mean a big step forward in the child's development. Overcoming illness is not generally considered a developmental step, beyond acquiring a lifelong immunity to the disease. However, surprisingly, many parents can describe exactly how their child changed as a result of the sickness. This can be related to potty-training, speech development or other developmental areas. Parents often describe how the childhood disease put an end to a period of listlessness and being generally under the weather, for which they couldn't find an explanation. This view can give a balanced insight into inoculations (see our other book, *Baby's First Year*).

Childhood diseases are briefly discussed below, along with any complications that may arise. Inoculations campaigns often focus on the potential complications of childhood diseases, which gives a distorted picture of their real danger, while the side effects of inoculations are underestimated. In relative terms, complications arise in a very low percentage of children who have the following diseases. However, this doesn't make them any less serious for those affected, so it's important to be aware of them.

When using the term 'childhood diseases' we refer to a specific group of diseases, which have become rare because of the inoculation programme. These are infectious diseases that particularly affect children: diphtheria, whooping cough, polio, measles, mumps, German measles (rubella), meningitis, chicken pox, scarlet fever, slapped-cheek syndrome and roseola. Your child can be inoculated for the first seven diseases listed below (up to and including meningitis) (see p. 133).

Diptheria

Diptheria is extremely rare in the UK due to the childhood immunization programme. The bacteria still exists around the world and most new cases are picked up abroad.

Whooping cough

Whooping cough still occurs quite often, in various degrees of severity, and can appear in children who have been inoculated. It is an infectious disease and can affect both children and adults who have come into contact with an infected patient.

Usually a child with whooping cough will seem healthy during the daytime. The characteristic fits of coughing come on particularly at night. The child may have a number of very severe coughing fits with wheezy breathing, in which she appears to almost choke. At the end of the attack the child often has to vomit. This also means the end of the coughing fit and then the child can relax again. Once the fit has passed, the child goes back to sleep quite easily, but the parents on the other hand have broken nights for several weeks. The best way to cope is to take turns sleeping with the child. For a small child over the age of one, whooping cough is quite a challenge for the whole family, but generally it's not a dangerous disease. However you should consult a doctor.

The period of contagion is long and lasts from one week before to three weeks after the start of the attacks. The incubation period is seven to ten days. Complications that can arise include middle-ear infections and pneumonia, but these are rare.

Tetanus

This isn't really a childhood disease. You can be infected throughout your life, especially after being injured in an accident or bitten by animals. Children can be inoculated against tetanus during their first years of life.

Polio (infantile paralysis)

This disease has been greatly reduced in the UK and only occurs in children who have not been inoculated. It's an inflammation of the nervous system, and in five per cent of the cases it leads to paralysis and related deformities of the limbs and/or torso.

Measles

Measles is one of the 'red spot diseases.' After a few days of a cold and fever, the fever disappears. The child appears to be getting better, but a few days later becomes really ill again, with a fever and wet red, enflamed eyes, so that she cannot tolerate light. There is a lot of mucus and the child coughs with a wet, gravelly cough. At the same time more and more red spots appear on the body. At first the spots are small, but by the second day they are already larger and then they merge together in large red patches and gradually disappear. This process comes to an end after ten days when the child is better, although it should be taken into account that he'll be very vulnerable for at least another week.

Measles is very contagious and is the result of direct contact between children. The incubation period is between ten and twelve days.

Occasionally there are complications in the form of middle-ear infections or pneumonia. One very rare complication can affect the brain, which can be life-threatening in the longer term.

Mumps

This is a harmless childhood disease, although older children and adults who contract it can become very ill. The parotid glands (usually both) are inflamed and there may be a passing irritation of the cerebral membrane.

It is not a very contagious disease and is only passed on through direct contact. Patients are contagious from a few days before the start of the symptoms until the glandular swelling has disappeared. The incubation period is from twelve to twenty-four days.

Complications: in older boys or men there may be a rare complication in the form of the inflammation of the epididymis. In a small proportion of cases, this complication can result in reduced fertility.

German measles (rubella)

This is a 'red spot disease' that is not always easy to diagnose because there are so few symptoms. Small red dots start behind the ears and gradually spread all over the body. The lymph nodes at the back of the head are almost always swollen. It is a harmless disease although there are sometimes passing complaints in the joints.

It is not very contagious. A patient is contagious from one week before the symptoms to one week after the start of the red spots. The incubation period is between twelve and twenty-one days.

Complications: if a pregnant woman catches German measles during the first three months of pregnancy, it can lead to damage in the baby's brain and sensory organs. Therefore it's a good idea for any women trying to get pregnant who have not had German measles to be inoculated a few months before.

Meningitis

There are several different strains of meningitis and a rough distinc-

tion can be made between inflammations caused by a virus and those caused by bacteria. Meningitis with a viral origin is virtually always cured without causing any damage. The bacterial type can lead to complications. The HIB vaccine was developed to protect against the strain of meningitis caused by the haemophilus influenza bacteria, which can lead to serious complications during the baby's first year. In rare cases, the pneumococcal bacteria can also cause meningitis during the first years of life and a vaccination it is now offered to infants.

The greatest risk of meningitis is over after the first year, although it doesn't pass entirely. For this reason, the meningococcal C vaccination is given at around twelve months.

If your child has a fever, you should look for the symptoms of meningitis. The first symptoms are similar to flu, but the child soon becomes seriously ill with a high fever. She may be drowsy and confused. Symptoms that should ring alarm bells are: stiffness of the neck, pain when moving the head forward and small bruises on the skin. Any one of these symptoms is a reason to go to the doctor immediately.

Chicken pox

Chicken pox usually starts as a cold with a fever and small red spots. The first clear blisters soon appear: they contain moisture, are between 2–6 mm ($^1/_8$–$^1/_4$ in) in diameter and are usually itchy. The spots and blisters develop one after the other and can also occur in the mouth and throat. The blisters break open, become crusts and gradually get better. Large blisters can sometimes leave a scar.

Chicken pox is very contagious and is passed through direct contact. People who spend time with the child can also transmit the disease, though this can sometimes be prevented by simply going outside to 'blow it away' for a few minutes. The patient is contagious from one day before the appearance of the spots until all the blisters have dried up. The incubation period is between fourteen and twenty-one days.

No significant complications are known.

Scarlet fever

Scarlet fever develops after a particular type of throat infection. After a few days of fever (when the child is usually sick once) red spots appear on the face, particularly on the cheeks, leaving a space without spots around the mouth. The child has glowing, dry eyes and a sore throat. On about the third day, spots also appear on the child's torso and limbs. After the disease, the hands and feet often start to peel. Adults who are infected by the child may have a throat infection. In that case, look out for the complications mentioned below, which can also occur in adults. The child does not devel-op a lifelong immunity to infections with the same bacteria after this disease, so she can contract it several times.

It is not very contagious. The incubation period is between one and seven days. There are quite a few complications with scarlet fever: inflammation of the heart and cardiac valves, acute rheumatism (inflammation of the joints), kidney infection and St Vitus' dance, in which, due to inflammation of the brain, the child starts to walk with a strange dancing gait. These complications are relatively rare but were common before the arrival of penicillin.

Slapped-cheek syndrome (fifth disease)

This is not a very striking disease and is rather like German measles. The only real symptom is the appearance of small red circles spread over the torso. Sometimes the child has a raised temperature. It is known as 'fifth disease' because it is the fifth most common disease characterized by a rash in children.

The incubation period is between seven and seventeen days. There are no known complications.

Roseola (sixth disease)

This is a completely harmless disease. It is particularly common in young children. After three to five days of a high fever for which there is no other obvious reason and which barely makes the child ill, the fever disappears and small red spots appear, starting on the torso and moving to the arms and legs.

The incubation period is between seven and fourteen days. Once a child has had this disease she acquires lifelong immunity. There are no known complications.

Vaccinations

In most English language speaking countries, the immunization programme is comprised of vaccines against the following diseases: diptheria, tetanus, whooping cough, polio, haemophilus influenza type B (Hib), as well as meningitis, measles, mumps and German measles (rubella). The programme varies in different countries and is regularly revised. The decision whether or not to inoculate a child, and if so for which diseases, is usually made in the first year of life, and we have included a more detailed overview in our other book, *Baby's First Year*.

If the regular programme of inoculations is followed, in the baby's first year in the UK a child is vaccinated against diphtheria, tetanus, whooping cough, polio and Hib (DTaP/IPV/Hib) all in one injection. She is given the pneumococcal vaccine (PCV) to protect against meningitis and the meningitis C vaccine (MenC) in separate injections. At around thirteen months old she will receive a vaccination against measles, mumps and rubella (MMR) all in one injection. Before starting school, she is given a pre-school booster inoculation of DTaP/IPV and MMR.

Every parent has a free choice with regard to vaccinations. In *Baby's First Year* we offered some points of view that may help parents to make their own decision about whether or not to immunize their children. After consideration, often together with the family doctor or at the child health centre, parents may decide on a different programme of inoculations, adapted to the child and in line with their own beliefs.

For a more detailed discussion, see *Baby's First Year*.

Looking after sick children

The first chapter of this book mentioned the importance of always giving a child plenty of time, and this certainly applies when she's ill. In order to recover properly the child needs the time, peace and quiet to be really ill and then to get properly better. Obviously this is easier said than done, because sickness is almost always inconvenient, and having a sick child requires a lot of energy from the parents.

As a parent, you have to remember that a toddler will regularly be ill and you will have to think in advance of ways to deal with this. This preparation will make all the difference when the child really does become ill, and it should make it possible to turn the period of sickness into a special and intimate time.

For a child it's helpful if there are a number of fixed habits related to being ill. For example, if she has a fever she can lie downstairs in a sleeping bag on the sofa or on a camp bed, and once she's slightly better again, she can walk around dressed warmly in a ski suit or something similar. In principle we follow the rule: stay in bed with a fever, then spend one day indoors when the fever has gone and then another at home after that. If a child has had one of the childhood diseases she may need a little bit longer to get better. In that case you should go with your instinct in deciding the right moment for her to join the daily routine again. Children need a particularly long period of recovery after scarlet fever, measles and whooping cough.

In addition, when the child is ill, it's also reassuring if there can be a number of fixed times during the day when being alone and spending time together, distraction and a period of calm alternate at regular intervals. Obviously the emphasis will depend on how sick the child feels. Being read to and doing craftwork together are good activities for a sick child.

A fever and eating properly do not go together well. It won't hurt if the child doesn't eat or hardly eats for a few days; obviously it's good to drink a lot, preferably in this case (slightly sweetened) herbal tea. Also make sure that the child does not become constipated as this can delay the healing process.

When a child no longer has a fever but doesn't really feel better yet, she often wants to do more than she really can do. This is difficult, both for the child because she is still so vulnerable, and for the parents. In that case, also try to incorporate a few clear times in the day to give the child support. It helps to have a box of favourite toys or new toys at hand.

If a child is sick for a long time or if several children become ill one after the other, you may feel like you're going up the wall. Try and be as prepared as possible to allow yourself some time out to restore your energy.

Rickets

Our body makes vitamin C when the sun shines on the skin. Vitamin D is necessary to build a good, strong skeleton. If there is a deficiency this can result in changes in the bones, first of all the ribs, the wrists and the ankles (thickening of the growth plate) or the bones of the skull can become soft. Symptoms are: a stubborn cold, muscular weakness and excessive perspiration. If the disease occurs during the period when teeth are forming, this can lead to a defect in the enamel of the permanent teeth. Rickets used to be common in children in Victorian times, but now the condition is rare in the UK.

Allergies

If a child often has tummy ache and diarrhoea or eczema, or often has a runny nose or is congested, she may be over-sensitive or allergic to something in her diet or in the environment. The reaction will always affect the outer limits of body parts: the intestinal mucus membrane, the skin or the mucus membrane of the respiratory tract. There are always two factors which play a role: something is introduced from the outside and there is a violent (internal) reaction, which attempts to keep this external agent outside. This reaction is provided by the immune system in the child's body.

Over-sensitivity and allergies appear to be becoming increasingly common. One reason for this could be that the (environmental) pollution of the ground, water and air, with which we come into contact in all sorts of ways without knowing it, constantly stimulates the immune system to a slight extent so that over-sensitivities develop. Increased sensitivity can also result, for example, after traumas during pregnancy or during the first years of life, and emotional events in the child's environment.

It's not always easy to determine whether there really is an allergy. A person can become over-sensitive to an enormous number of things. You can only really be certain if this applies by eliminating and provoking possible causes. This means that the compaint improves if the substance is omitted and/or deteriorates when it is brought back into use. When the cause is known, the general advice is to avoid contact with it for the time being.

However, this approach tackles only one aspect of the matter. This is because the 'inside' also plays a central role, and it can help to ensure that the immune system is calmed down and not over-stimulated. This involves avoiding possible undesirable stimuli, both at the physical and at the psychological level; it is well known that the immune system can be affected by both physical and psychological stimuli.

First of all, there are possibilities at a material level in the choice of foods. Organic and biodynamic farming deliberately avoid the use of pesticides, which eliminates some undesirable stimuli. At the psychological level there are also various possibilities. A child has to assimilate and 'digest' everything she experiences through her senses psychologically. There should only be a certain amount every day to avoid undigested experiences turning into problems. In many cases, a great deal of improvement can be achieved by avoiding impressions made from hearing the radio or watching TV, but also, for example, by not going shopping in very busy places.

Over-sensitivity is a problem of limits; the consistent use of limits in the child's upbringing also has a positive effect. If parents use limits sensibly themselves and radiate a sense of calm, this can have a miraculous effect. When this calm is established, the violent reaction of over-sensitivity often declines.

In addition to introducing calm into an over-stimulated situation, it's important to strengthen the healthy digestive and assimilative capacity of the child. This is good for every child, but in particular for a child who tends to be over-sensitive, because it has some preventative effect. As indicated earlier, real and genuine sensory impressions help (for example, no flavourings or colourants in foodstuffs), as well as a rhythmic pattern to the day, to which the body and psyche can relate. For example, if meals are eaten at the same time every day, the digestive system adapts to this.

Eating problems

Many children are fussy eaters during the toddler years, particularly with regard to hot meals and especially when eating green vegetables. The extent to which this becomes a problem is different for every child.

A great deal will have already been achieved if you have got into the routine of a daily family meal with a clear beginning and end. When a problem does arise it's good to ask yourself a number of questions first:

• Is the child becoming ill?

• Is the meal too late and therefore the child too tired?

• Was the child given too much on her plate?

• Is the child basically a morning or an evening person?

• Are there any tensions in her environment?

• Does the child not have an appetite?

• Is she just in a 'no' phase?

Usually conflict arises because the child is going through a stubborn phase and she expresses this through her eating behaviour. Not eating is a very effective weapon. As the person responsible for the child's upbringing, you find it difficult to tolerate that a carefully prepared meal, intended to keep your child alive, simply disappears into the bin. This means that eating becomes a loaded matter. A child can be hyper-aware of this and this certainly does not help her appetite.

The child is asking you to be creative and flexible. You can try all sorts of tricks like 'one bite for you and one for me,' or making combinations, for example, of carrots with yogurt in one dish, or a bite of pudding and a bite of vegetables one after the other. Hiding the vegetables that are being refused in savoury cookies (see p. 111) or puréed soups can also often help. It's not always easy to do this in a playful way and at the same time feel confident that it will work.

It's a good idea to remember that there are many different causes for this problem and there are many different ways of looking at it. You'll be able to get further advice at your child health centre.

Sleeping problems

For some children, going to sleep or sleeping through the night is a big problem, and the advice given in this book for the different stages may not be adequate. Usually the problem arises as a result of bad habits. This requires a didactic approach, not medication in the first instance. At most, some anthroposophical medicines can support the process.

When tackling a stubborn sleeping problem it's a good idea to first ask yourself the question whether it really is a problem for you that your child finds it difficult to go to sleep or wakes up at night, or whether other people have talked you into believing this. Whether your approach will work is directly related to your own motivation. For example, if you know rationally that a child should sleep at night but you don't really think it's such a problem in your heart of hearts, you will almost certainly lack the strength to remain resolute. Breaking down

sleeping habits takes a lot of effort and sometimes pain, as the child can resist violently and the process is often accompanied by tears. If you don't want to confront the problems, while you're suffering from difficult evenings or broken nights, it's a good idea to examine what's stopping you. Often there can be influences affecting you that you are unaware of. It's possible that people around you have a big influence on you, or that these ideas are the result of your own (negative) experiences as a child. These could have caused you to believe that you should always be there for your child, even at night, because you would otherwise be a bad parent; or that your child will suffer from a permanent trauma if she was left to cry at night. Feelings of guilt because you were unable to spend enough time with your child during the daytime can also play a role. These sorts of thoughts are often not very practical, because no parent can ever be there for their child at all times in the long term, least of all, a totally exhausted parent. If these sorts of ideas are getting in your way, you should try and do something about them — if necessary with some help.

If the sleeping problems arise in combination with health concerns, it's a good idea to go to the child health centre or family doctor first. Then you can look together at the most suitable approach for your child.

If moving house or tensions in the family play a role in the sleeping problem, it's possible to look for an approach that will put as little pressure on your child as possible. If the problems are really serious, this is often only possible to a certain extent, despite your good intentions. If your child is frightened, it's important to weigh up whether the sleeping problems or the fear should be tackled first and which needs the most urgent attention.

Once the decision has been taken to really do something about the problems, the emphasis, in the first instance, is on the daytime. A number of indications were given on p. 41 under the heading *The toddler's three weapons*. Sometimes these immediately have a good effect and they usually create the conditions for success later on.

When you then tackle the evening and nights, the important thing is that you feel confident about your approach, and that both parents adopt the same line.

The starting point for all the different methods is that you cannot force a child to sleep, but you can insist that she stays in bed and allows the other members of the family to have their sleep.

Make sure that there's a clear evening ritual and then very firmly tell your child she is going to sleep and that everyone else is going to sleep until the start of another day. The intonation of your voice will make it clear to your child that you are very serious about this. One method could be to stop responding to the crying. At most you could go into the room to see whether the child is lying comfortably. The first evening or night the child may cry for a few hours, and after that he'll cry for some evenings but not others. However, within a week nearly all healthy children simply sleep through the night. Another method is to go to the child when she's crying, show your face for a moment, quietly tell her she must go to sleep and repeat this at consistent moments until the child is asleep. With this method most children also sleep through the night within a week.

The child will certainly revert to her old behaviour from time to time, but by intervening appropriately, everyone's sleep can soon be ensured.

Behavioural problems

At any age a child's conduct can reveal behavioural or psychological problems. We mention a number of symptoms here that may give you reason to consult the family doctor. The symptoms mentioned here do not actually mean there is a problem; this can only be determined with further examination.

Hyperactivity

Hyperactivity applies if a child can never sit still, touches everything, is restless and excited and her attention is constantly drawn to different objects or events.

Anxiety

Abnormal anxiety applies when a child is very shy, makes huge scenes about nothing, becomes totally panicky, for example, when she sees the doctor, or gets worked up into a state where you can no longer get through to him.

Egocentrism

In this case the child is only concerned with herself. She seems to live in her own little bubble and doesn't appear to notice her surroundings. She barely moves about and doesn't really take part in any social life.

Aggression

Some children display excessively destructive behaviour, where everything around them ends up broken or demolished. It's as though the child enjoys this element of destruction. She is drawn like a magnet to a situation where something can be broken and appears to be incorrigible in this respect.

The above characteristics are approximate descriptions. They serve only to make you more aware of the possibility of behavioural problems so that you can seek help in time if necessary.

Appendix

Procedures

Camomile tummy wrap

Camomile tummy wrap

Make camomile tea with a handful of camomile flowers and pour on half a litre (half quart) of water that has just gone off the boil. Leave the tea to brew for ten minutes.

Make sure that the child is lying in bed in his pyjamas and that his feet are warm. If necessary, give him a flat hot-water bottle that isn't too hot.

For the tummy wrap use a cotton cloth or a piece of silk of approximately 10 x 75 cm (4 x 30 in) and roll it up.

Use a nappy or tea towel to wring out the cloth: place the roll in the nappy or tea towel and roll up the whole thing so that there are two dry ends to take hold of (see illustration on previous page).

Take a woollen shawl or blanket, which is larger than the tummy wrap, and place it under the child's back.

Now place the rolled up 'sausage' in a bowl or dish with the ends over the edge (see illustration on previous page). Pour the camomile tea over this through a tea strainer so that the cloth absorbs as much as possible. Hold the dry ends of the tea towel with both hands and wring out the wrap very firmly. Remove the inner cloth from the wringing towel only when the child's tummy is exposed. It's important that the cloth is hot and that steam rises from it, but it should no longer feel soaking wet.

Wrap the cloth quickly around the child's tummy and then immediately cover it with the woollen shawl so that as little heat as possible is lost. If necessary, hold the woollen shawl in place with a safety pin. Pull the pyjama top down over it and the pyjama trousers up over it. A flat warm hot-water bottle on the tummy will keep the wrap pleasantly warm.

Making a tummy wrap requires skilful hands. It has to be done quickly so that it retains its heat. A compress is often advised instead because it's simpler.

Now leave the child to doze off. After half an hour the wrap can be removed, but this is not necessary if the child is asleep.

Camomile tummy compress

Carry out the camomile tea preparations as described above for the camomile tummy wrap.

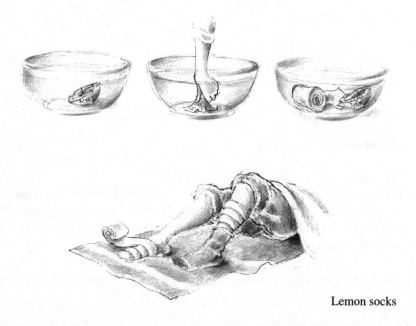

Lemon socks

Take a square cloth, for example, a handkerchief, and fold it in half twice into a square. Place the compress in a wringing cloth (as above) and soak the whole thing in the camomile tea, with the ends hanging over the edge so they remain dry. Wring out the compress firmly and then place it on the tummy, keeping it as hot as possible.

Immediately wrap a woollen shawl or blanket around the child's body so that it becomes a warm package. Two light but warm hot-water bottles can be placed against the sides, on the right and left.

Leave the child to doze off to sleep. After half an hour the compress can be removed, but this is not necessary if the child is asleep.

Lemon socks

Squeeze half a lemon into a bowl of warm water with the palm of your hand. Soak a bandage in the lemon water. Wring out the bandage thoroughly with a cloth (as described above) and wrap it around the child's feet and lower legs. Then put woollen socks over the top.

Make sure that the child has warm feet — if necessary place a hot-water bottle at the bottom of the bed.

These lemon socks should only be used for a high fever. In the case of a very high temperature the socks may be steamed dry by the child in ten to fifteen minutes. If so, the procedure could be repeated twice more, followed by a break of at least half an hour. Usually the fever will then be reduced and the child will have gone to sleep.

There is no point in the fever being brought below 38° C (100° F) because the positive effects of the fever are then undone (see p. 119).

If you have no lemons in the house, you could use a tablespoon of vinegar instead.

Onion compress

Finely chop a medium-sized onion and place it in the middle of a handkerchief. Fold up the package and secure it with elastoplast. Heat up the compress on the radiator or a hot-water bottle until it reaches body temperature and place it behind the child's earlobe. Hold the compress

Onion compress

in place with a hat or a headscarf. The onion opens up the nasal passages and within a few minutes will reduce the pain of an ear infection.

Hot bandage

Take a cloth at least as large as the area that needs to be kept warm and dampen it with hot water (a tea towel is suitable for a neck bandage). Apply the bandage to the desired place and cover it well to retain as much heat as possible. This bandage can be left for quite a long time and if necessary can be moistened again.

Ice compress

Place some ice cubes in a plastic sandwich bag. As a safeguard, place another plastic bag around it. Break up the ice cubes and gently dab the painful place.

Physiological salt

Dissolve a teaspoon of salt in a glass of tepid water. Use a pipette to put drops of the salt water in the nose.

Camomile nose drops

Dissolve one teaspoon of salt in a glass of boiling water. Put some camomile flowers into a paper coffee filter and submerge it in the water until it becomes a pale yellow colour. Put the nose drops in a clean pipette bottle and refresh every two days. Use the nose drops lukewarm.

Product Information

Food

Apple (pear) molasses: Syrup made by condensing apple (pear) syrup; when you buy this make sure that no other sugar or syrup has been added.

Barley malt syrup: Syrup made by malting barley; makes food more easily digestible and has a laxative effect.

Bulgar wheat: An easily digestible cereal made from wheat; of Turkish origin.

Cereal flakes: Buy cereal flakes in small quantities to ensure they stay fresh. Suitable flakes include rice, buckwheat, millet, oats and barley flakes.

Cheese: Use very mild cheese.

Concentrate: Concentrated fruit juice without any additions like added sugar.

Corn malt syrup: A natural sweetener made by malting corn and barley.

Couscous: An easily digestible cereal made of wheat; of Moroccan origin.

Herbal tea: (Mixtures of) lime blossom, jasmine, lemon balm, thyme, rosehip, liquorice, apple peel, fennel, aniseed and peppermint (in moderation) are suitable.

Honey: Use good quality, unheated honey.

Millet: An easily digestible cereal.

Fruit juice concentrate: Fruit syrup without any other additions; to be used as a sweetener, or greatly diluted as juice.

Nuts: Almonds and hazelnuts, ground or in the form of a paste to spread on bread, are particularly suitable for small children.

Oil: Use a cold-pressed oil with a neutral taste, such as sunflower or safflower oil.

Quark (curd cheese): When quark is mentioned in this book, it always refers to full fat quark.

Quinoa: This barley-like seed is easily digestible and good to use as an additional cereal.

Raw sugar: Unrefined cane sugar.

Sour milk products: The following are suitable: yogurt, buttermilk and viili.

Wherever possible, use ingredients of organic or biodynamic quality (Demeter label). All these products are available in health-food shops and sometimes in supermarkets.

Medication

Arnica ointment 10% (Weleda)
Arnica D3 (internal) (Weleda)
Arnica essence 20% (Weleda)
Calendula ointment (Weleda)
Calendula essence (Weleda)
Combudoron gel for burns (Weleda)
Combudoron ointment for burns (Weleda)
Combudoron liquid for burns (Weleda)
Combudoron spray
Menthol powder (from a chemist or pharmacy)
Nose cream (Wala or Weleda)
Norit/birch charcoal/carbo betulae powder (Weleda or from a pharmacy)
Witch hazel

Bibliography

Health and sickness

Bentheim, T van, *Home Nursing for Carers,* Floris Books, Edinburgh 2006.

Bie, Guus van der and Huber, Machteld, *Foundations of Anthroposophical Medicine,* Floris Books, Edinburgh 2003.

Bott, Victor, *Anthroposophical Medicine,* Anthroposophic Press, New York.

Bühler, Walter, *Living with your Body: the Body as an Instrument of the Soul,* Rudolf Steiner Press, London.

Evans, Michael and Rodger, Iain, *Healing for Body, Soul: An Introduction to Anthroposophical Medicine,* Floris Books, Edinburgh 2000. In USA published as *Complete Healing,* Steinerbooks, New York 2007.

Glöcker, Michaela and Goebel, Wolfgang, *A Guide to Child Health,* Floris Books, Edinburgh, 2007.

Holtzapfel, Walter, *Children's Destinies: the Three Directions of Human Development,* Mercury Press, New York.

Holtzapfel, Walter, *Our Children's Illnesses,* Mercury Press, New York.

Husemann, Armin, *The Harmony of the Human Body,* Floris Books, Edinburgh 2002.

Leroi, Rita, *Illness and Healing,* Temple Lodge Press, London.

Leviton, Richard, *Anthroposophic Medicine Today,* Anthroposophic Press, New York.

Mees, L.F.S, *Blessed by Illness,* Anthroposophic Press, New York.

Steiner, Rudolf, *Introducing Anthroposophical Medicine,* Anthroposophical Press, New York.

Steiner, Rudolf, and Ita Wegman, *The Fundamentals of Therapy,* Rudolf Steiner Press, London.

Studer, Hans-Peter and Douch, Geoffrey, *Vaccination: A Guide for Making Personal Choices,* Floris Books, Edinburgh 2004.

Twentyman, Ralph, *The Science and Art of Healing,* Floris Books, Edinburgh 1992.

Wolff, Otto, *Anthroposophically Orientated Medicine and its Remedies,* Mercury Press, New York.

Wolff, Otto, *Home Remedies,* Floris Books, Edinburgh 2000.

Parenting & general education

Anschütz, Marieke, *Children and their Temperaments,* Floris Books, Edinburgh 1995.

Parent Network, *Being a Parent,* Hawthorn Press, Stroud.

Britz-Crecelius, Heidi, *Children at Play,* Inner Traditions, Vermont.

Dunn, Judy, and Plomin, Robert. *Separate Lives: Why Siblings Are So Different,* Basic Books, 1990.

Harwood, A.C. *The Way of a Child,* Sophia Books, Forest Row.

Kane, Franklin G., *Parents as People: the Family as a Creative Process,* Aurora, Edmonton.

Kiel-Hinrichsen, Monika, *Why Children don't Listen,* Floris Books, Edinburgh 2006.

König, Karl, *Brothers and Sisters: the Order of Birth in the Family,* Floris Books, Edinburgh.

König, Karl, *The First Three Years of the Child,* Floris Books, Edinburgh 1998.

Large, Martin, *Who's Bringing Them Up?: Television and Child Development,* Hawthorn Press, Stroud.

Maslow, Abraham H. *Motivation and Personality,* Harper & Row, New York, 1987.

Needleman, H. L., and P. J. Landrigan, *Raising Children Toxic Free,* Farrar, Straus & Giroux, New York 1994.

Pearce, Joseph Chilton, *The Magical Child,* Bantam, New York.

Salter, Joan, *The Incarnating Child,* Hawthorn Press, Stroud.

Toys, activities & festivals

Barz, Brigitte, *Festivals with Children,* Floris Books, Edinburgh 1987.

Berger, Petra, *Feltcraft: Making Dolls, Gifts and Toys*, Floris Books, Edinburgh 1994.

Marion, Isabel, *Christmas in the Family*, Floris Books, Edinburgh 2006

Neuschütz, Karin, *Sewing Dolls*, Floris Books, Edinburgh 2009.

Reinckens, Sunnhild, *Making Dolls*, Floris Books, Edinburgh 2003.

Wolk-Gerche, Angelika, *Creative Felt: Felting and Making Toys and Gifts,* Floris Books, Edinburgh 2009

Picture books, board books & nursery rhymes

Beskow, Elsa, *Emily and Daisy*, Floris Books, Edinburgh 2009.

Beskow, Elsa, *Pelle's New Suit*, Floris Books, Edinburgh 1989.

Drescher, Daniela, *What's Hiding in There?* Floris Books, Edinburgh 2008.

Klaassen Sandra, *Uan the Little Lamb*, Floris Books, Edinburgh 2006.

Koopmans Loek, *Any Room for Me?* Floris Books, Edinburgh 1992.

Lines, Kathleen and Jones, Harold, *Lavender's Blue: A Book of Nursery Rhymes*, Oxford University Press, 2004.

Muller, Gerda, *Spring; Summer; Autumn; Winter* (board books), Floris Books, Edinburgh 1994.

Olfers, Sibylle von, *Princess in the Forest*, Floris Books, Edinburgh 1994.

Olfers, Sibylle von, *The Story of the Snow Children*, Floris Books, Edinburgh 2005.

Price, Rebecca, *Toby and the Flood* (about bedwetting), Floris Books, Edinburgh 2008.

Wenz-Viëtor, *The Christmas Angels*, Floris Books, Edinburgh 2008.

Useful Organizations

Immunization

Government recommended schedules

UK: www.immunisation.nhs.uk
Ireland: www.immunisation.ie
USA: http://mchb.hrsa.gov/mchirc/chusa
Canada: www.phac-aspc.gc.ca
Australia: www.mydr.com.au
New Zealand: www.immune.org.nz
South Africa: www.capegateway.gov.za

Anthroposophical medicine

International
Anthroposophical Society Medical
Section, Goetheanum, 4143 Dornach,
Switzerland
Tel: +41-61-706 4290
Fax: +41-61-706 4291
Email: am@medsektion-goetheanum.ch
www.medsektion-goetheanum.org

Physicians' Association for
Anthroposophic Medicine (PAAM)
1923 Geddes Ave, Ann Arbor MI48104
Tel: 734-930-9462 Fax: 734-662-1727
Email: paam@anthroposophy.org
www.paam.net

The Anthroposophical Medical
Association
53 Cainscross Road, Stroud GL5 4EX
Tel: 01453-762 151
Email: medical.section@yahoo.co.uk

Park Attwood Clinic
Trimpley, Bewdley, Worcs. DY12 1RE
Tel: 01299-861 444 Fax: 01299-861 375
www.parkattwood.org

Weleda UK
Heanor Road, Ilkeston DE7 8DR
Tel: 0115-944 8222
Fax: 0115-944 8210
Email: Weleda.direct@weleda.co.uk
www.weleda.co.uk

Weleda US
PO Box 675, Palisades NY 10964
Tel: 800-241-1030
Fax: 800-280-4899
Email: info@weleda.com
http://usa.weleda.com

Weleda New Zealand
302 Te Mata Road, Havelock North
Tel. 0800-802 174
Fax: 0800-804 989
Email: weleda@weleda.co.nz
www.weleda.co.nz

Weleda Australia
Tel: 03-9723 7278
Email: weleda@weleda.com.au

Pharma Natura (South Africa)
PO Box 494, Bergvlei 2012
Tel: 011-445 6000 Fax: 011-445 6089
Email: healthcare@pharma.co.za
www.pharma.co.za

Index

Paulien Bom and Machteld Huber

Baby's First Year

Growth and Development from 0 to 12 Months

A baby's first year presents parents with a variety of challenges. The initial excitement of pregnancy is followed by the child's birth and subsequent development, but many parents feel in need of significant support and information regarding the more mundane areas of daily life, such as nutrition.

This practical guide takes a holistic approach to the growth and development of a baby. Written by doctors qualified in both conventional and anthroposophical medicine, it deals with all aspects of the care of a small child up to the age of twelve months. Broken down into short comprehensive chapters spanning different periods of development, it covers subjects such as feeding and growth, diet and weaning, bathing and sleeping. It also includes sections on physical and spiritual development, and presents an overview of childhood vaccinations.

www.florisbooks.co.uk

Michaela Glöckler & Wolfgang Goebel

A Guide to Child Health

Third Edition

Now in its third edition, this revised and updated guide to children's physical, psychological and spiritual development combines medical advice with issues of upbringing and education.

Throughout, the book is extremely practical, covering all childhood illnesses, ailments and conditions, and home nursing. The authors also outline the connection between education and healing, with all that this implies for the upbringing and good health of children. Medical, educational and religious questions often overlap, and in the search for the meaning of illness it is necessary to study the child as a whole — as body, soul and spirit.

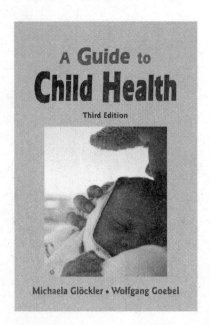

'A vital book for parents who seek a deeper understanding of their child's health. 'The Green Parent Favourite' award.'
—*The Green Parent*

'Full of the kind of wise tips that used to get passed down from mother to daughter but are sadly missing in this day and age. An invaluable reference source. Highly recommended.'
— *Juno: A natural approach to family life*

www.florisbooks.co.uk